Power Notes

Getting a clear view of the big picture

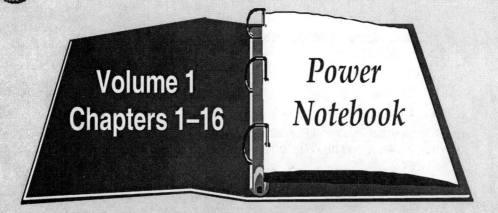

**Volume 1
Chapters 1–16**

*Power
Notebook*

A Teaching and Learning System
for use with
ACCOUNTING
Warren, Reeve, Fess 19e

South-Western Publishing

John Wanlass – Interactive Learning

Accounting Team Director: Richard Lindgren
Senior Acquisitions Editor: David L. Shaut
Senior Marketing Manager: Sharon Oblinger
Senior Developmental Editor: Ken Martin
Production Editor: Mark Sears

Copyright © 1999
by South-Western College Publishing
Cincinnati, Ohio

International Thomson Publishing
South-Western is an ITP Company. The ITP trademark is used under license.

Portions of the material in all chapters copyrighted by John W. Wanlass, 1999.

ISBN: 0-538-87419-8

   3 4 5 6 7   GP   4 3 2 1 0 9

Printed in the United States of America

Power Notes

For the Student – Questions and Answers

Question .... **What is Power Notes and what does it include?**

Answer .... Power Notes is a teaching/learning package designed to be used with your textbook, **Accounting**, 19e, by Carl S. Warren, James M. Reeve, and Philip E. Fess. It includes the following:

1. A Power Notebook for the student.
2. Presentation Transparencies and PowerPoint®[1] slides for the instructor.

These components cover topics from your textbook and are designed to maximize your classroom note taking opportunities as well as provide a chapter review.

Question .... **How can I effectively use the Power Notebook?**

Answer .... The Power Notebook is designed to be used during a classroom discussion of accounting topics. It includes reduced copies of your presentation transparencies and PowerPoint slides. In some cases you will be challenged to complete sections or answer questions. Exercises which relate to specific topics are noted to the right of the reduced picture. After you finish your study of the chapter topics, complete the review questions.

Question .... **How is the Power Notebook used with other available resources?**

Answer .... The Power Notebook is designed to be used with your textbook and Working Papers Plus. Together these three resources provide a complete learning package. These resources combine the best of in-class and individual study as shown below.

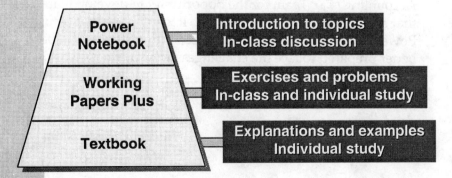

1. PowerPoint is a registered trademark of Microsoft Corporation. Any reference to PowerPoint refers to this footnote.

For the Instructor – Questions and Answers

Question .... What are the instructor components in the Power Notes package?

Answer .... Power Notes includes two components for the instructor:

1. Presentation transparencies, which include all of the topics in the student's Power Notebook.

2. PowerPoint slides for use with Microsoft's PowerPoint presentation program. These are a dynamic version of the Power Notebook and the presentation transparencies.

Question .... How can I effectively use Power Notes in the classroom?

Answer .... Here are a few ideas we have found to be effective.

1. The Power Notebook includes critical-thinking questions and other challenges. Some of these are included in the presentation transparencies and some are not. Review the Power Notebook before presenting the transparencies or slides.

2. Some of the Power Notebook exhibits are incomplete. Challenge the student to complete these sections before showing the answers.

3. Introduce a topic using the transparency or slide and then challenge the student to complete a related exercise, using the Notebook as a guide.

Acknowledgments

Power Notes is the result of many years of development and experimentation in the classroom. The contributions of accounting faculty and students have greatly influenced this project. I am indebted to the South-Western College Accounting/Tax Team for the opportunity to develop materials that enhance accounting education. It is my hope that by using Power Notes you will enjoy your accounting studies and be better prepared to face the challenges of the business world.

John Wanlass

Interactive Learning

Power Notebook

ACCOUNTING
Warren, Reeve, Fess, 19e

Brief Contents – Volume 1

Power Notebook
Solutions for Review Questions

Chapter 1	Chapter 2	Chapter 3	Chapter 4	Chapter 5	Chapter 6
N1 - 13	**N2 - 13**	**N3 - 14**	**N4 - 10**	**N5 - 14**	**N6 - 10**
1. F	1. F	1. T	1. T	1. F	1. T
2. T	2. F	2. F	2. F	2. T	2. F
3. T	3. F	3. T	3. F	3. T	3. F
4. T	4. T	4. T	4. F	4. F	4. T
5. F	5. F	5. T	5. T	5. T	5. F
6. F	6. T	6. F	6. F	6. T	6. T
7. F	7. F	7. T	7. T	7. F	7. F
8. F	8. F	8. F	8. F	8. T	8. F
9. T	9. F	9. F	9. F	9. T	9. F
10. F	10. F		10. T	10. F	10. T
11. F	11. F	**N3 - 15**	11. F	11. T	11. F
	12. F		12. T	12. F	12. F
N1 - 14	13. T	1. B	13. F		13. T
	14. T	2. C	14. F	**N5 - 15**	14. F
1. B		3. A			
2. D	**N2 - 14**	4. D	**N4 - 11**	1. D	**N6 - 11**
3. B		5. A		2. C	
4. D	1. B		1. C	3. B	1. D
5. C	2. D		2. A	4. A	2. B
6. B	3. B		3. A	5. C	3. C
	4. C		4. C	6. D	4. C
	5. D		5. B	7. D	5. D
	6. D		6. B	8. C	6. C
			7. B		7. D
			8. C		8. D

Power Notebook
Solutions for Review Questions

Chapter 7	Chapter 8	Chapter 9	Chapter 10	Chapter 11	Chapter 12
N7 - 8	**N8 - 12**	**N9 - 13**	**N10 - 15**	**N11 - 9**	**N12 - 14**
1. T	1. T	1. T	1. T	1. T	1. T
2. F	2. F	2. T	2. T	2. T	2. F
3. T	3. F	3. F	3. T	3. F	3. F
4. F	4. F	4. T	4. T	4. F	4. F
5. F	5. F	5. F	5. F	5. T	5. T
6. F	6. T	6. F	6. F	6. T	6. F
7. T	7. F	7. F	7. T	7. T	7. F
8. T	8. T	8. F	8. F	8. F	8. F
9. T	9. T	9. F	9. F	9. T	9. F
10. T	10. T	10. T	10. F	10. F	10. T
11. F	11. F	11. F	11. T	11. F	11. T
12. T	12. F	12. F	12. F	12. F	12. F
		13. T	13. F	13. F	13. T
N7 - 9	**N8 - 13**	14. F	14. F		14. F
1. C	1. C		15. F	**N11 - 10**	
2. A	2. B	**N9 - 14**	16. T	1. A	**N12 - 15**
3. B	3. A			2. C	1. D
4. B	4. B	1. A	**N10 - 16**	3. D	2. B
5. B	5. C	2. B		4. A	3. C
6. D	6. C	3. B	1. B	5. B	4. B
7. C	7. C	4. C	2. A	6. A	5. A
	8. D	5. C	3. B		6. D
	9. D	6. D	4. B		7. B
			5. C		8. C
			6. D		

Power Notebook
Solutions for Review Questions

Chapter 13	Chapter 14	Chapter 15	Chapter 16
N13 - 11	**N14 - 14**	**N15 - 17**	**N16 - 13**
1. F	1. F	1. F	1. T
2. T	2. T	2. F	2. T
3. T	3. T	3. T	3. F
4. F	4. T	4. F	4. T
5. T	5. F	5. F	5. F
6. T	6. T	6. T	6. F
7. F	7. T	7. T	7. T
8. F	8. T	8. F	8. T
9. T	9. F	9. F	9. F
10. T	10. F	10. T	10. T
	11. T	11. F	11. F
N13 - 12	12. T	12. T	12. T
	13. F	13. T	13. F
1. C	14. T	14. T	
2. A			**N16 - 14**
3. C	**N14 - 15**	**N15 - 18**	
4. A			1. D
5. B	1. D	1. A	2. B
6. D	2. B	2. C	3. C
	3. A	3. B	4. C
	4. B	4. D	5. A
	5. A	5. C	6. D
	6. C	6. C	7. B
	7. B	7. C	
	8. A	8. A	
	9. D		
	10. A		

Learning Objectives

1. Nature of a Business
2. The Role of Accounting in Business
3. Business Ethics
4. Profession of Accounting
5. Generally Accepted Accounting Principles
6. Assets, Liabilities, and Owner's Equity
7. Business Transactions
8. Financial Statements
9. Financial Analysis and Interpretation

C1

Power Note Topics

- Accounting – An Information Process
- Users of Accounting Information
- Profession of Accounting
- The Accounting Equation
- Business Transactions
- Financial Statements
- Ratio of Liabilities to Owner's Equity

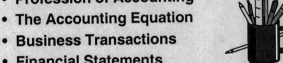

Notes:

Accounting — An Information Process

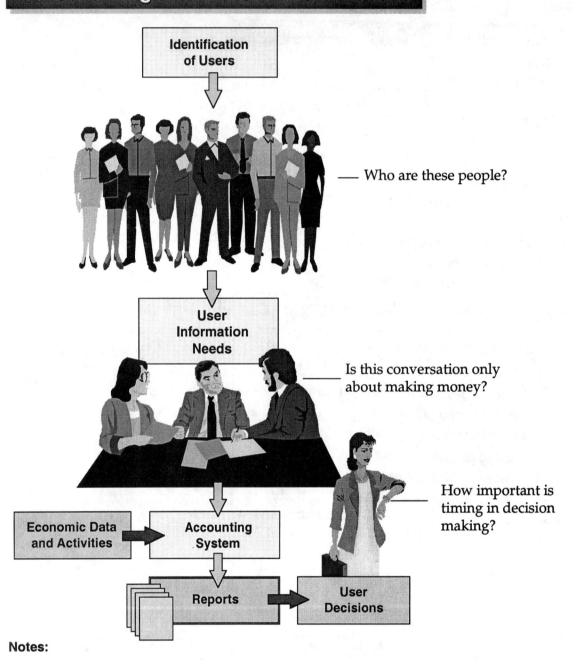

Identification of Users

— Who are these people?

User Information Needs

— Is this conversation only about making money?

How important is timing in decision making?

Economic Data and Activities → Accounting System

Reports → User Decisions

Notes:

Users of Accounting Information

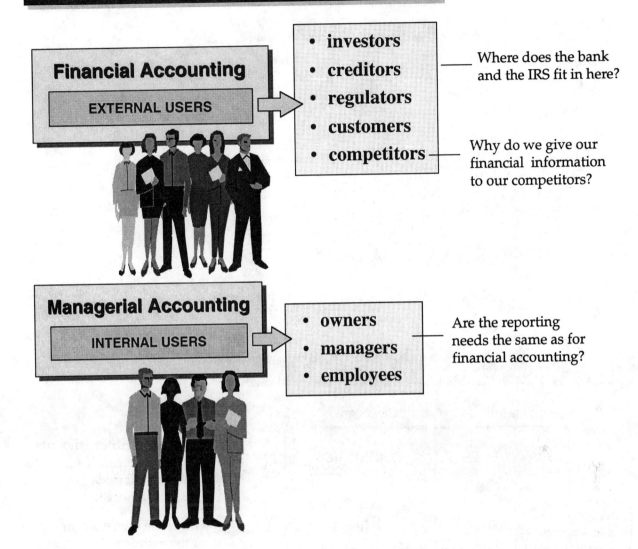

Financial Accounting

EXTERNAL USERS

- **investors**
- **creditors**
- **regulators**
- **customers**
- **competitors**

Where does the bank and the IRS fit in here?

Why do we give our financial information to our competitors?

Managerial Accounting

INTERNAL USERS

- **owners**
- **managers**
- **employees**

Are the reporting needs the same as for financial accounting?

Notes:

The Accounting Profession

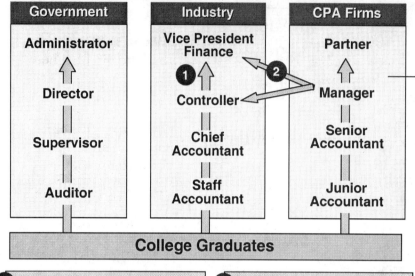

Does this mean that 1 year in public accounting is equal to 2 or 3 years in industry?

The Accounting Equation

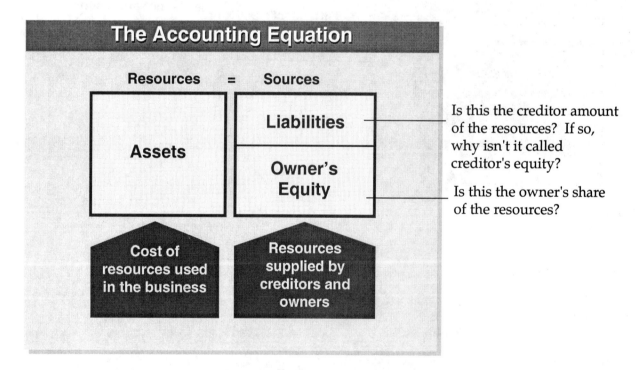

Is this the creditor amount of the resources? If so, why isn't it called creditor's equity?

Is this the owner's share of the resources?

How would a delivery van with a cost of $20,000 and a balance owed of $15,000 be reflected in the accounting equation?

Business Transactions

a. Pat King deposits $15,000 in a bank account for Computer King.

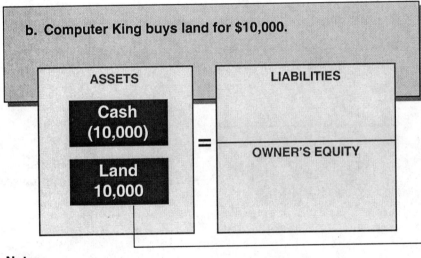

ASSETS		LIABILITIES
Cash **15,000**	**=**	
		OWNER'S EQUITY
		Pat King, Capital **15,000**

Does it matter where Pat got the $15,000 to invest?

Is this still Pat's cash or is it now owned by Computer King?

b. Computer King buys land for $10,000.

ASSETS		LIABILITIES
Cash **(10,000)**	**=**	
		OWNER'S EQUITY
Land **10,000**		

Notes:

Why did the company pay cash? Isn't it better to buy property by giving a note payable?

Business Transactions

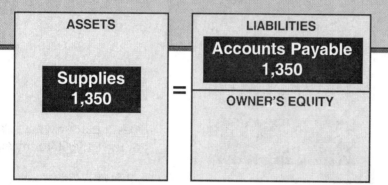

c. Computer King buys supplies for $1,350, agreeing to pay the supplier in the near future.

ASSETS		LIABILITIES
		Accounts Payable 1,350
Supplies 1,350	=	OWNER'S EQUITY

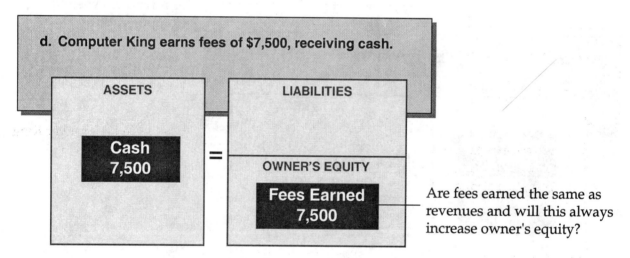

d. Computer King earns fees of $7,500, receiving cash.

ASSETS		LIABILITIES
Cash 7,500	=	OWNER'S EQUITY
		Fees Earned 7,500

Are fees earned the same as revenues and will this always increase owner's equity?

Notes:

Business Transactions

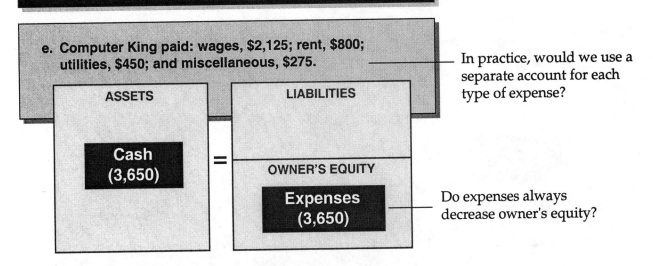

e. Computer King paid: wages, $2,125; rent, $800; utilities, $450; and miscellaneous, $275.

In practice, would we use a separate account for each type of expense?

ASSETS		LIABILITIES
Cash (3,650)	=	
		OWNER'S EQUITY
		Expenses (3,650)

Do expenses always decrease owner's equity?

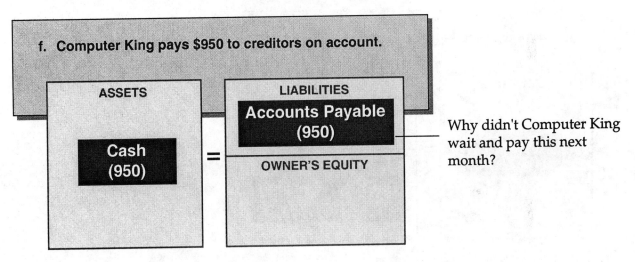

f. Computer King pays $950 to creditors on account.

ASSETS		LIABILITIES
		Accounts Payable (950)
Cash (950)	=	OWNER'S EQUITY

Why didn't Computer King wait and pay this next month?

Notes:

Business Transactions

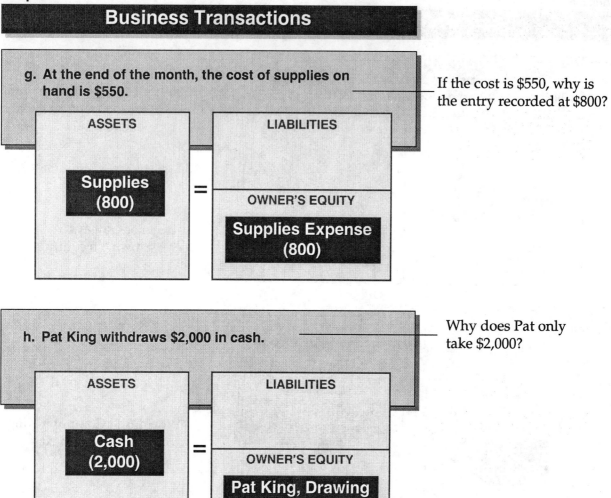

g. At the end of the month, the cost of supplies on hand is $550.

If the cost is $550, why is the entry recorded at $800?

ASSETS = LIABILITIES

Supplies (800)

OWNER'S EQUITY

Supplies Expense (800)

h. Pat King withdraws $2,000 in cash.

Why does Pat only take $2,000?

ASSETS = LIABILITIES

Cash (2,000)

OWNER'S EQUITY

Pat King, Drawing (2,000)

Notes:

Transaction Summary

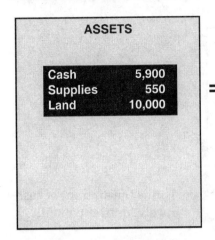

ASSETS	
Cash	5,900
Supplies	550
Land	10,000

=

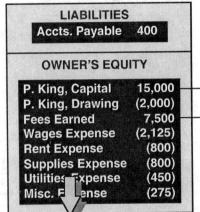

LIABILITIES	
Accts. Payable	400
OWNER'S EQUITY	
P. King, Capital	15,000
P. King, Drawing	(2,000)
Fees Earned	7,500
Wages Expense	(2,125)
Rent Expense	(800)
Supplies Expense	(800)
Utilities Expense	(450)
Misc. Expense	(275)

Do investments and revenue <u>both</u> increase owner's equity?

Effects of Transactions on Owner's Equity

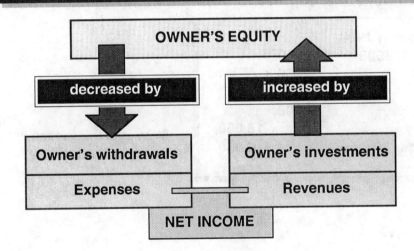

OWNER'S EQUITY

decreased by — Owner's withdrawals — Expenses

increased by — Owner's investments — Revenues

NET INCOME

Calculate the following :

Assets .... _____

Liabilities .... _____

Ending Owner's Equity .... _____

Net Income .... _____

Computer King
Income Statement
For the Month Ended November 30, 1999

Fees earned		$7,500
Operating expenses:		
Wages expense	$2,125	
Rent expense	800	
Supplies expense	800	
Utilities expense	450	
Miscellaneous expense	275	
Total operating expenses		4,450
Net income		$3,050

Is this the amount of cash received for the month?

Computer King
Statement of Owner's Equity
For the Month Ended November 30, 1999

Pat King, capital, November 1, 1999		$ 0
Investment on November 1, 1999	$15,000	
Net income for November	3,050	
	$18,050	
Less withdrawals	2,000	
Increase in owner's equity		16,050
Pat King, capital, November 30, 1999		$16,050

Why isn't this the same as the total assets?

Notes:

Computer King
Balance Sheet
November 30, 1999

Assets		
Cash	$5,900	
Supplies	550	
Land	10,000	
Total assets		$16,450
Liabilities		
Accounts payable	$ 400	
Owner's Equity		
Pat King, capital	16,050	
Total liabilities and owner's equity		$16,450

Where does this number come from?

Computer King
Statement of Cash Flows
For the Month Ended November 30, 1999

Cash flows from operating activities:		
Cash received from customers	$ 7,500	
Deduct cash payments for expenses and payments to creditors	4,600	
Net cash flow from operating activities		$ 2,900
Cash flows from investing activities:		
Cash payments for acquisition of land		(10,000)
Cash flows from financing activities:		
Cash received as owner's investment	$15,000	
Deduct cash withdrawal by owner	2,000	
Net cash flow from financing activities		13,000
Net cash flow and Nov. 30, 1999 cash balance		$5,900

Is this always the same as the Balance Sheet cash account?

Ratio of Liabilities to Owner's Equity

Objective: Use the ratio of liabilities to owner's equity to analyze the ability of a business to withstand poor business conditions and to pay its creditors.

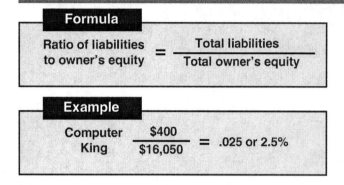

Formula

$$\text{Ratio of liabilities to owner's equity} = \frac{\text{Total liabilities}}{\text{Total owner's equity}}$$

Example

Computer King $\dfrac{\$400}{\$16,050} = .025 \text{ or } 2.5\%$

Notes:

True / False Questions

True   False

_____ _____   1. The excess of the revenue over the expenses incurred in earning the revenue is called a net loss.

_____ _____   2. A business transaction is the occurrence of an event or of a condition that must be recorded.

_____ _____   3. A separate legal entity, organized in accordance with state or federal statutes and in which ownership is divided into shares of stock, is referred to as a corporation.

_____ _____   4. Equities in the assets of a business may be subdivided into rights of creditors and rights of owners.

_____ _____   5. Accountants who render accounting services on a fee basis, and staff accountants employed by them, are said to be engaged in private accounting.

_____ _____   6. A summary of the changes in the owner's equity of a business entity that have occurred during a specific period of time, such as a month or a year, is called a statement of cash flows.

_____ _____   7. A partnership is owned by not less than four individuals.

_____ _____   8. The financing activities section of the statement of cash flows includes cash transactions that enter into the determination of net income.

_____ _____   9. Accounting is often characterized as the "language of business."

_____ _____ 10. A claim against a customer for sales made on credit is an account payable.

_____ _____ 11. If total assets decreased by $30,000 during a specific period and owner's equity decreased by $35,000 during the same period, the period's change in total liabilities was a $10,000 decrease.

Instructions:

Place a check mark in the appropriate column.

____ 1. Assets are:
   a. a part of the accounting equation only after they are paid for
   b. financed by the owner and/or creditors
   c. the same as expenses because they are acquired with cash
   d. the same as net worth

____ 2. The business entity concept means that:
   a. the owner is part of the business entity
   b. an entity is organized according to state or federal statutes
   c. an entity is organized according to the rules set by the FASB
   d. the entity is an individual economic unit for which data are recorded

____ 3. Which of the following is NOT a business transaction?
   a. render services
   b. sign a contract for future services
   c. receive cash for services to be rendered later
   d. pay for supplies

____ 4. Properties owned by a business are referred to as:
   a. owner's equity
   b. liabilities
   c. equities
   d. assets

____ 5. If total liabilities increased by $20,000 during a period of time and owner's equity increased by $5,000 during the same period, the amount and direction (increase or decrease) of the period's change in total assets is:
   a. $20,000 increase
   b. $20,000 decrease
   c. $25,000 increase
   d. $25,000 decrease

____ 6. If beginning capital was $45,000, ending capital is $40,000, and the owner's withdrawals were $25,000, the amount of net income or net loss was:
   a. net income of $30,000
   b. net income of $20,000
   c. net loss of $5,000
   d. net income of $25,000

Instructions:

Enter the letter of the best answer in the space provided.

Power Notes

Analyzing Transactions

Learning Objectives

1. Usefulness of an Account
2. Characteristics of an Account
3. Analyzing and Summarizing Transactions
4. Illustration of Analyzing and Summarizing
5. Trial Balance
6. Discovery and Correction of Errors
7. Financial Analysis and Interpretation

C2

Power Note Topics

- **Double-Entry Accounting**
- **Analyzing and Recording Transactions**
- **Chart of Accounts, Trial Balance**
- **Journal, Ledger, and Trial Balance**
- **Recording and Posting an Entry**
- **Correcting Errors**
- **Horizontal Analysis**

Notes:

Double-Entry Accounting

" Double-entry accounting is based on a
simple concept: each party in a business
transaction will receive something and give
something in return. In bookkeeping terms,
what is received is a debit and what is given
is a credit. The T account is a representation
of a scale or balance."

Who is Luca Pacioli?
When did he develop
this system?

**Luca Pacioli
Developer of
Double-Entry
Accounting**

Scale or Balance

**Receive
DEBIT**   **Give
CREDIT**

T account

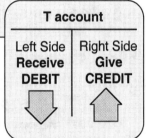

Left Side Receive DEBIT	Right Side Give CREDIT

Expanded Accounting Equation

" The basic accounting equation can be
expanded to include all five financial categories
indicating what has been received and given."

Are there only
five categories?

**Luca Pacioli
Father of the
Balance Sheet**

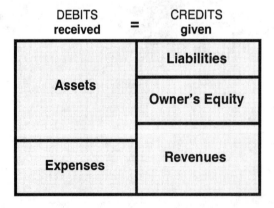

DEBITS received	=	CREDITS given
Assets		Liabilities
		Owner's Equity
Expenses		Revenues

Write the expanded accounting equation formula.

Using Luca Pacioli's model above, shade the
area which shows the amount of net income.

Computer King
A Sole Proprietorship

" On November 1, 1999, I started a sole proprietorship called Computer King. I plan to use my knowledge of microcomputers and offer computer consulting services for a fee. The following double-entry transations show how amounts received (debits) always equal amounts given (credits)."

Pat King, Owner

Entry A.

Pat King deposits $15,000 in a bank account for Computer King.

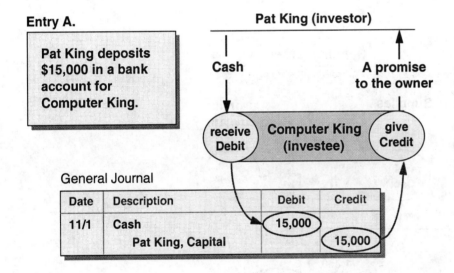

General Journal

Date	Description	Debit	Credit
11/1	Cash	15,000	
	Pat King, Capital		15,000

Notes:

Entry B.

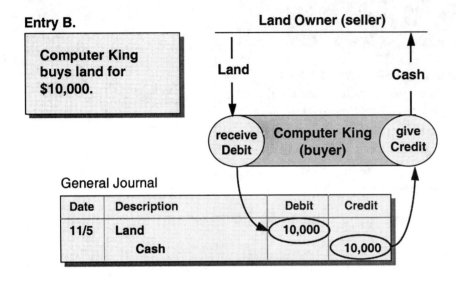

Computer King
buys land for
$10,000.

Land Owner (seller)

Land

Cash

receive
Debit

Computer King
(buyer)

give
Credit

General Journal

Date	Description	Debit	Credit
11/5	Land	10,000	
	Cash		10,000

Entry C.

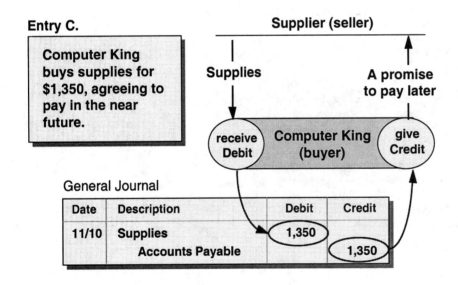

Computer King
buys supplies for
$1,350, agreeing to
pay in the near
future.

Supplier (seller)

Supplies

A promise
to pay later

receive
Debit

Computer King
(buyer)

give
Credit

General Journal

Date	Description	Debit	Credit
11/10	Supplies	1,350	
	Accounts Payable		1,350

Notes:

Chapter 2

Entry D.

Computer King earns fees of $7,500, receiving cash.

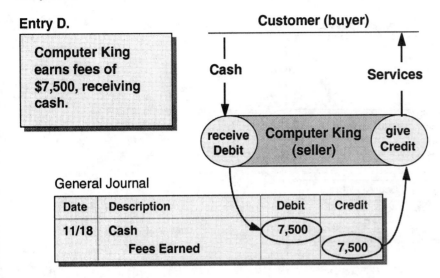

Customer (buyer)

Cash   Services

receive Debit | **Computer King (seller)** | give Credit

General Journal

Date	Description	Debit	Credit
11/18	Cash	7,500	
	Fees Earned		7,500

Entry E.

Computer King paid: wages, $2,125; rent, $800; utilities, $450; and miscellaneous, $275.

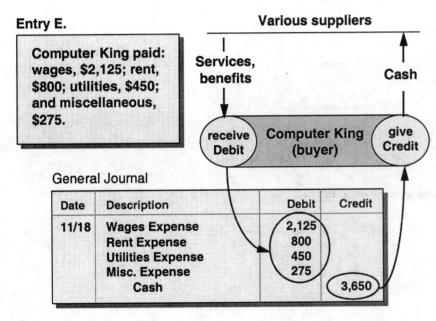

Various suppliers

Services, benefits   Cash

receive Debit | **Computer King (buyer)** | give Credit

General Journal

Date	Description	Debit	Credit
11/18	Wages Expense	2,125	
	Rent Expense	800	
	Utilities Expense	450	
	Misc. Expense	275	
	Cash		3,650

Notes:

Entry F.

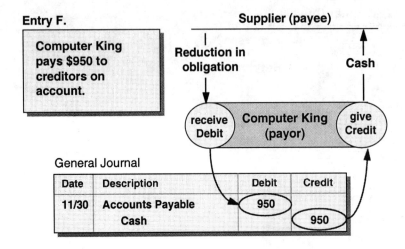

Entry G.

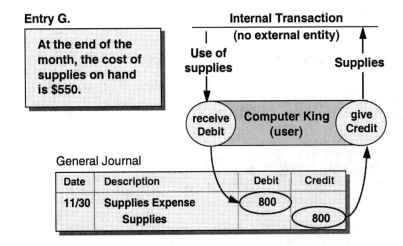

Notes:

Entry H.

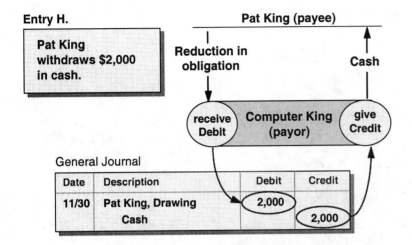

Pat King withdraws $2,000 in cash.

General Journal

Date	Description	Debit	Credit
11/30	Pat King, Drawing	2,000	
	Cash		2,000

Transaction Summary

Debits / received = Credits / given

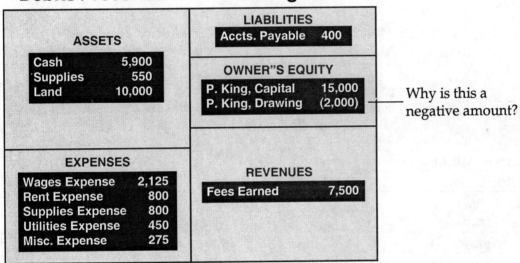

ASSETS

Cash	5,900
Supplies	550
Land	10,000

LIABILITIES

Accts. Payable	400

OWNER"S EQUITY

P. King, Capital	15,000
P. King, Drawing	(2,000)

Why is this a negative amount?

EXPENSES

Wages Expense	2,125
Rent Expense	800
Supplies Expense	800
Utilities Expense	450
Misc. Expense	275

REVENUES

Fees Earned	7,500

Notes:

Computer King
Chart of Accounts

Balance Sheet	Income Statement
1. Assets	**4. Revenue**
11 Cash	41 Fees Earned
12 Accounts Receivable	
14 Supplies	**5. Expenses**
15 Prepaid Insurance	51 Wages Expense
17 Land	52 Rent Expense
18 Office Equipment	54 Utilities Expense
	55 Supplies Expense
2. Liabilities	59 Miscellaneous Expense
21 Accounts Payable	
23 Unearned Rent	
3. Owner's Equity	
31 Pat King, Capital	
32 Pat King, Drawing	

If I want to add an account between wages and rent, what number would I use?

Computer King
Trial Balance
November 30, 1999

11	Cash	5,900	
14	Supplies	550	
17	Land	10,000	
21	Accounts Payable		400
31	Pat King, Capital		15,000
32	Pat King, Drawing	2,000	
41	Fees Earned		7,500
51	Wages Expense	2,125	
52	Rent Expense	800	
54	Utilities Expense	450	
55	Supplies Expense	800	
59	Miscellaneous Expense	275	
		22,900	22,900

Balance Sheet

Income Statement

Calculate the following :

Total Assets .... _____

Total Liabilities .... _____

Ending Owner's Equity .... _____

Net Income .... _____

Journal, Ledger, Trial Balance

1. **Transactions are analyzed and recorded in journal.**

Documents   Journal

2. **Transactions are posted from journal to ledger.**

Journal   Ledger

3. **Trial balance is prepared.**

Trial Balance

Notes:

Recording and Posting an Entry

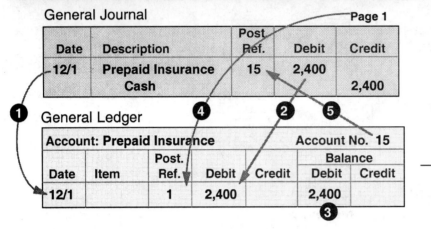

—— Posting the debit.

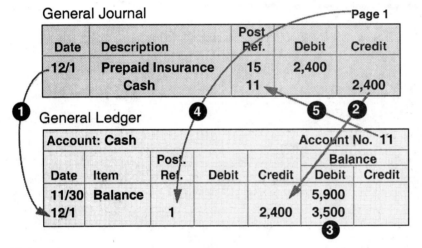

—— Posting the credit.

Notes:

Correcting Errors

Three Types of Errors

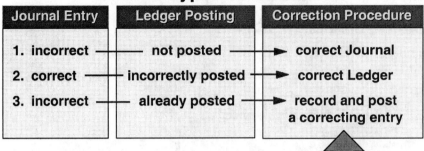

Journal Entry	Ledger Posting	Correction Procedure
1. incorrect	not posted	correct Journal
2. correct	incorrectly posted	correct Ledger
3. incorrect	already posted	record and post a correcting entry

Error 3 requires a correcting journal entry.

Correcting Errors – An Example

On May 5 a purchase of office equipment on account was incorrectly journalized and posted as shown.

General Journal – As recorded and posted

Date	Description	Debit	Credit
5/5	Supplies	12,500	
	Accounts Payable		12,500

General Journal – A correcting entry

Date	Description	Debit	Credit
5/5			

Record the appropriate correcting entry.

Financial Analysis and Interpretation

Objective: Use horizontal analysis to compare financial statements from different periods.

Comparative Balance Sheet
December 31, 2000 and 1999

Assets	2000	1999	Increase (Decrease) Amount	Percent
Current assets	$ 550,000	$ 533,000	$ 17,000	3.2%
Long-term investments				
Plant assets (net)				
Intangible assets				

Horizontal Analysis:

$$\frac{\text{Current year (2000)} \quad \$550,000}{\text{Base year (1999)} \quad \$533,000} = 103.2\%$$

$$\frac{\text{Increase amount} \quad \$17,000}{\text{Base year (1999)} \quad \$533,000} = 3.2\%$$

Comparative Income Statement
December 31, 2000 and 1999

	2000	1999	Increase (Decrease) Amount	Percent
Sales	$1,530,500	$1,234,000	$296,500	24.0%
Sales returns	32,500	34,000	(1,500)	(4.4%)
Net sales	$1,498,000	$1,200,000	$298,000	24.8%
Cost of goods sold				
Gross profit				

Horizontal Analysis:

$$\frac{\text{Current year (2000)} \quad \$1,498,000}{\text{Base year (1999)} \quad \$1,200,000} = 124.8\%$$

$$\frac{\text{Increase amount} \quad \$298,000}{\text{Base year (1999)} \quad \$1,200,000} = 24.8\%$$

Notes:

True / False Questions

_____ _____ 1. A recording error caused by the erroneous rearrangement of digits, such as writing $864 as $846, is called a slide.

_____ _____ 2. A group of accounts for a business entity is called a journal.

_____ _____ 3. Every business transaction affects a minimum of one account.

_____ _____ 4. The difference between the total debits and the total credits posted to an account yields a figure called the balance of the account.

_____ _____ 5. Amounts entered on the left side of an account, regardless of the account title, are called credits or charges to the account.

_____ _____ 6. The residual claim against the assets of a business after the total liabilities are deducted is called owner's equity.

_____ _____ 7. The process of recording a transaction in a journal is called posting.

_____ _____ 8. A listing of the accounts and balances from a ledger is called a chart of accounts.

_____ _____ 9. Net worth is a commonly used term for liabilities.

_____ _____ 10. Posting a transaction twice will cause the trial balance totals to be unequal.

_____ _____ 11. Journalizing is the process of entering amounts in the ledger.

_____ _____ 12. The erroneous moving of an entire number one or more spaces to the right or left, such as writing $450 as $45, is called a transposition.

_____ _____ 13. Expense accounts are increased by debits.

_____ _____ 14. A proof of the equality of debits and credits in the ledger at the end of an accounting period is called a trial balance.

Instructions:

Place a check mark in the appropriate column.

Multiple Choice Questions

____ 1. When a payment is made to a supplier for goods previously purchased on account, the debit is to:
   a. an asset account
   b. a liability account
   c. a capital account
   d. an expense account

____ 2. When rent is prepaid for several months in advance, the debit is to:
   a. an expense account
   b. a capital account
   c. a liability account
   d. an asset account

____ 3. Credits to Cash result in:
   a. an increase in owner's equity
   b. a decrease in assets
   c. an increase in liabilities
   d. an increase in revenue

____ 4. The equality of debits and credits in the ledger should be verified at the end of each accounting period by preparing a(n):
   a. accounting statement
   b. balance report
   c. trial balance
   d. account verification report

____ 5. The first step in recording a transaction in a two-column journal is to:
   a. write an explanation
   b. record the debit
   c. record the credit
   d. record the date

____ 6. The classification and normal balance of the drawing account is:
   a. a revenue with a credit balance
   b. an expense with a debit balance
   c. a liability with a credit balance
   d. owner's equity with a debit balance

Instructions:

Enter the letter of the best answer in the space provided.

Learning Objectives

1. **The Matching Concept**
2. **Nature of the Adjusting Process**
3. **Recording Adjusting Entries**
4. **Summary of Adjustment Process**
5. **Financial Analysis and Interpretation**

C3

Power Note Topics

- **Reporting Revenue and Expense**
- **The Matching Concept**
- **Trial Balance, Chart of Accounts**
- **Deferrals and Accruals**
- **Summary of Adjustments**
- **Vertical Analysis**

Notes:

Reporting Revenue and Expense

Cash Basis of Accounting

- ✔ **Revenue reported when cash is received**
- ✔ **Expense reported when cash is paid**
- ✔ **Does not properly match revenues and expenses** ——— Why not?

Accrual Basis of Accounting

- ✔ **Revenue reported when earned** ——— What does earned mean?
- ✔ **Expense reported when incurred** ——— What does incurred mean?
- ✔ **Properly matches revenues and expenses in determining net income**
- ✔ **Requires adjusting entries at end of period** ——— The focus of this chapter!
- ✔ **It just sounds mean – it really isn't** ——— A "cruel" method?

Notes:

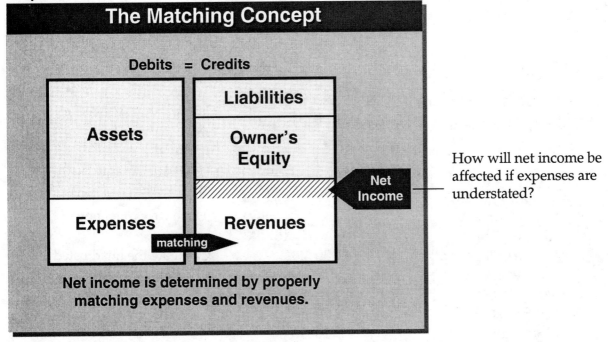

How will net income be affected if expenses are understated?

Using the accrual method of accounting:

When are revenues recorded?

When are expenses recorded?

	Computer King Unadjusted Trial Balance December 31, 1999		
11	Cash	2,065	
12	Accounts Receivable	2,220	
14	Supplies	2,000	
15	Prepaid Insurance	2,400	
17	Land	10,000	
18	Office Equipment	1,800	
21	Accounts Payable		900
23	Unearned Rent		360
31	Pat King, Capital		15,000
32	Pat King, Drawing	4,000	
41	Fees Earned		16,340
51	Wages Expense	4,275	
52	Rent Expense	1,600	
54	Utilities Expense	985	
55	Supplies Expense	800	
59	Miscellaneous Expense	455	
		32,600	32,600

Is this balance correct at year end?

How much of this has been used?

Have we earned any of this?

Calculate the unadjusted net income.

Two different but very important questions:

Deferrals: Are there balances already on the books that need to be adjusted?

Accruals: Are there incurred expenses or earned revenues that are not yet recorded?

Computer King
Expanded Chart of Accounts

Balance Sheet	Income Statement
1. Assets	**4. Revenue**
11 Cash	41 Fees Earned
12 Accounts Receivable	42 Rent Revenue
14 Supplies	
15 Prepaid Insurance	**5. Expenses**
17 Land	51 Wages Expense
18 Office Equipment	52 Rent Expense
19 Accumulated Depreciation	53 Depreciation Expense
	54 Utilities Expense
2. Liabilities	55 Supplies Expense
21 Accounts Payable	56 Insurance Expense
22 Wages Payable	59 Miscellaneous Expense
23 Unearned Rent	
3. Owner's Equity	
31 Pat King, Capital	
32 Pat King, Drawing	

Why do we need these five new accounts?

Adjustments – Deferrals and Accruals

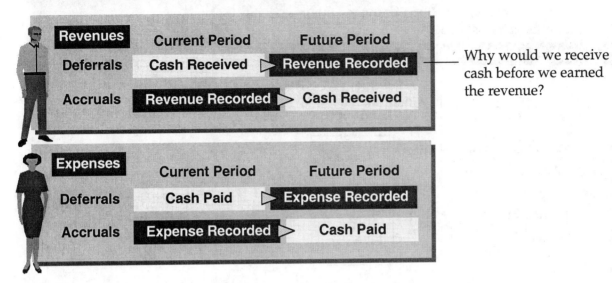

Why would we receive cash before we earned the revenue?

How are deferrals and accruals different?

Adjustments – Deferred Expense

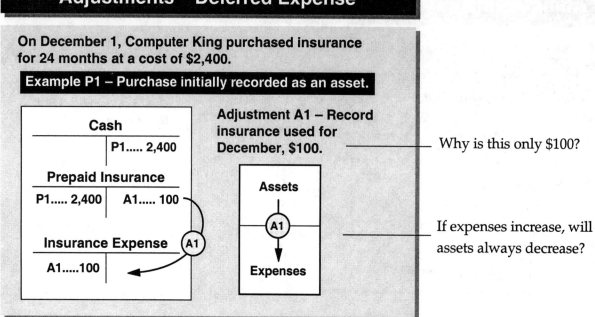

On December 1, Computer King purchased insurance for 24 months at a cost of $2,400.

Example P1 – Purchase initially recorded as an asset.

Cash

P1..... 2,400

Prepaid Insurance

P1..... 2,400 | A1..... 100

Insurance Expense (A1)

A1.....100

Adjustment A1 – Record insurance used for December, $100.

Assets
↓
(A1)
↓
Expenses

Why is this only $100?

If expenses increase, will assets always decrease?

How does this adjustment affect the:

Income Statement?

Balance Sheet?

What are the adjusted balances for:

Prepaid Insurance? ...._____

Insurance Expense? ...._____

Adjustments – Deferred Expense

On December 1, Computer King purchased insurance for 24 months at a cost of $2,400.

Example P2 – Purchase initially recorded as an expense.

Cash	
	P2..... 2,400

Prepaid Insurance	
A2..... 2,300	

Insurance Expense	
P2..... 2,400	A2.....2,300

Adjustment A2 – Record insurance unused as of December 31.

Assets

↑

A2

Expenses

How do you calculate the unused amount?

If expenses decrease, will assets always increase?

How does this adjustment affect the:

Income Statement?

Balance Sheet?

What are the adjusted balances for:

Prepaid Insurance? ...._____

Insurance Expense? ...._____

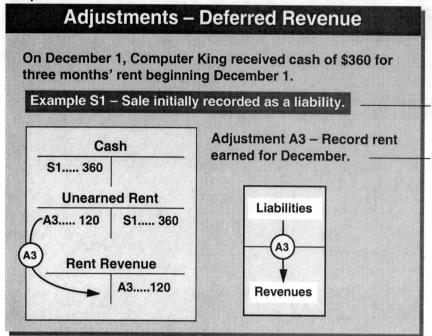

Adjustments – Deferred Revenue

On December 1, Computer King received cash of $360 for three months' rent beginning December 1.

Example S1 – Sale initially recorded as a liability.

Adjustment A3 – Record rent earned for December.

Why is this recorded as a liability?

How do I calculate the amount earned?

Cash

S1..... 360

Unearned Rent

A3..... 120 | S1..... 360

A3

Rent Revenue

A3.....120

Liabilities

A3

Revenues

How does this adjustment affect the:

Income Statement?

Balance Sheet?

What are the adjusted balances for:

Unearned Rent?....................._____

Rent Income? ...._____

Adjustments – Deferred Revenue

On December 1, Computer King received cash of $360 for three months' rent beginning December 1.

Example S2 – Sale initially recorded as revenue.

Why is this recorded as revenue?

Adjustment A4 – Record rent unearned as of December 31.

How do I calculate how much is unearned at December 31?

Cash	
S2..... 360	

Unearned Rent	
	A4..... 240

(A4)

Rent Revenue	
A4..... 240	S2.....360

Liabilities

↑

(A4)

Revenues

How does this adjustment affect the:

Income Statement?

Balance Sheet?

What are the adjusted balances for:

Unearned Rent? ...._____

Rent Income? ...._____

Adjustments – Accrued Expense

Computer King received employee services for the last two days of December amounting to $250, to be paid later.

Adjustment A5 – Record accrued wages of $250. ———— Why do I have to record this if its not yet paid?

Wages Payable	
	A5..... 250

Wages Expense (A5)

Bal.....4,275	
A5.....250	

Liabilities

↑

(A5)

↓

Expenses

Are liabilities and expenses both increased?

How does this adjustment affect the:

Income Statement?

Balance Sheet?

What are the adjusted balances for:

Wages Payable? ...._____

Wages Expense? ...._____

Adjustments – Accrued Revenue

As of December 31, Computer King provided 25 hours of services at $20 per hour to be billed next month.

Adjustment A6 – Record accrued fees earned of $500.

How will the financial statements be affected if I wait and record this later when cash is received?

Accounts Receivable
Bal.....2,220
A6..... 500

Fees Earned
Bal....16,340
A6.....500

A6

Assets

A6

Revenues

Are assets and revenues <u>both</u> increased?

How does this adjustment affect the:

Income Statement?

Balance Sheet?

What are the adjusted balances for:

Accounts Receivable? ...._____

Fees Earned? ...._____

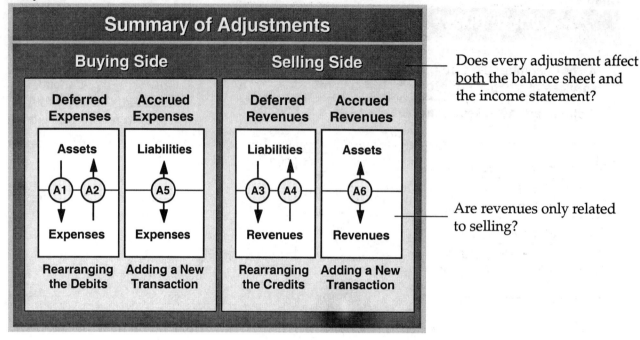

Does every adjustment affect <u>both</u> the balance sheet and the income statement?

Are revenues only related to selling?

Which of the adjustments increase net income? Why?

Which of the adjustments decrease net income? Why?

Financial Analysis and Interpretation

Objective: Use vertical analysis to compare financial statement items with each other and with industry averages.

Comparative Income Statements
For the Years Ended December 31, 2000 and 2001

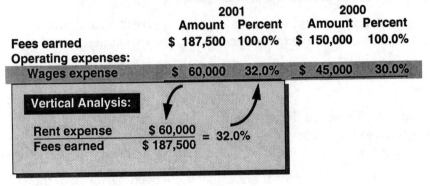

	2001		2000	
	Amount	Percent	Amount	Percent
Fees earned	$ 187,500	100.0%	$ 150,000	100.0%
Operating expenses:				
Wages expense	$ 60,000	32.0%	$ 45,000	30.0%

Vertical Analysis:

$$\frac{\text{Rent expense } \$ 60,000}{\text{Fees earned } \$ 187,500} = 32.0\%$$

Notes:

True / False Questions

True   False

True	False		
_____	_____	1.	Most businesses use the accrual basis of accounting.
_____	_____	2.	When the reduction in prepaid expenses is not properly recorded, this causes the asset accounts and expense accounts to be overstated.
_____	_____	3.	Accumulated depreciation accounts may be referred to as contra asset accounts.
_____	_____	4.	The adjusting entry to record depreciation of fixed assets consists of a debit to a depreciation expense account and a credit to an accumulated depreciation account.
_____	_____	5.	When services are not paid for until after they have been performed, the accrued expense is recorded in the accounts by an adjusting entry at the end of the accounting period.
_____	_____	6.	A deferral is an expense that has not been paid or a revenue that has not been received.
_____	_____	7.	Accrued expenses may be described on the balance sheet as accrued liabilities.
_____	_____	8.	The amount of accrued revenue is recorded by debiting a liability account and crediting a revenue account.
_____	_____	9.	A contra asset account for land will normally appear in the fixed assets section of the balance sheet.

Instructions:

Place a check mark in the appropriate column.

Multiple Choice Questions

_____ 1. Entries required at the end of an accounting period to bring the accounts up to date and to ensure the proper matching of revenues and expenses are called:
   a. matching entries
   b. adjusting entries
   c. contra entries
   d. correcting entries

_____ 2. The decrease in usefulness of fixed assets as time passes is called:
   a. consumption
   b. deterioration
   c. depreciation
   d. contra asset

_____ 3. The difference between the fixed asset account and the related accumulated depreciation account is called the:
   a. book value of the asset
   b. fair market value of the asset
   c. net cost of the asset
   d. contra account balance of the asset

_____ 4. If a $250 adjustment for depreciation is not recorded, which of the following financial statement errors will occur?
   a. expenses will be overstated
   b. net income will be understated
   c. assets will be understated
   d. owner's equity will be overstated

_____ 5. The amount of accrued but unpaid expenses at the end of the fiscal period is both an expense and a(n):
   a. liability
   b. asset
   c. deferral
   d. revenue

Instructions:

Enter the letter of the best answer in the space provided.

Learning Objectives

1. Work Sheet
2. Financial Statements
3. Adjusting and Closing Entries
4. Fiscal Year
5. Accounting Cycle
6. Financial Analysis and Interpretation

C4

Power Note Topics

- The Work Sheet
- Financial Statements
- The Closing Process
- Post-Closing Trial Balance
- Accounting Cycles
- Working Capital and
   Current Ratio

Notes:

Computer King - Work Sheet - Two Months Ended 12/31/99

Account	Trial Balance Debit	Trial Balance Credit	Adjustments Debit	Adjustments Credit	Adj. Trial Balance Debit	Adj. Trial Balance Credit
11 Cash	2,065				2,065	
12 Accounts Receivable	2,220		(e) 500		2,720	
14 Supplies	2,000			(a) 1,240	760	
15 Prepaid Insurance	2,400			(b) 100	2,300	
17 Land	10,000				10,000	
18 Office Equipment	1,800				1,800	
19 Accumulated Depr.		0		(f) 50		50
21 Accounts Payable		900				900
22 Wages Payable		0		(d) 250		250
23 Unearned Rent		360	(c) 120			240
31 Pat King, Capital		15,000				15,000
32 Pat King, Drawing	4,000				4,000	
41 Fees Earned		16,340		(e) 500		16,840
42 Rent Revenue		0		(c) 120		120
51 Wages Expense	4,275		(d) 250		4,525	
52 Rent Expense	1,600				1,600	
53 Depreciation Expense	0		(f) 50		50	
54 Utilities Expense	985				985	
55 Supplies Expense	800		(a) 1,240		2,040	
56 Insurance Expense	0		(b) 100		100	
59 Misc. Expense	455				455	
	32,600	32,600	2,260	2,260	33,400	33,400

Notes:

Computer King - Work Sheet - Two Months Ended 12/31/99

Account	Adj. Trial Balance Debit	Credit	Income Statement Debit	Credit	Balance Sheet Debit	Credit
11 Cash	2,065				2,065	
12 Accounts Receivable	2,720				2,720	
14 Supplies	760				760	
15 Prepaid Insurance	2,300				2,300	
17 Land	10,000				10,000	
18 Office Equipment	1,800				1,800	
19 Accumulated Depr.		50				50
21 Accounts Payable		900				900
22 Wages Payable		250				250
23 Unearned Rent		240				240
31 Pat King, Capital		15,000				15,000
32 Pat King, Drawing	4,000				4,000	
41 Fees Earned		16,840		16,840		
42 Rent Revenue		120		120		
51 Wages Expense	4,525		4,525			
52 Rent Expense	1,600		1,600			
53 Depreciation Expense	50		50			
54 Utilities Expense	985		985			
55 Supplies Expense	2,040		2,040			
56 Insurance Expense	100		100			
59 Misc. Expense	455		455			
	33,400	33,400	9,755	16,960	23,645	16,440
Net Income			7,205			7,205
			16,960	16,960	23,645	23,645

Notes:

Computer King
Income Statement
For Two Months Ended December 31, 1999

Fees earned	$16,840	
Rent revenue	120	
Total revenues		$16,960
Expenses:		
Wages expense	$ 4,525	
Supplies expense	2,040	
Rent expense	1,600	
Utilities expense	985	
Insurance expense	100	
Depreciation expense	50	
Miscellaneous expense	455	
Total expenses		9,755
Net income		$ 7,205

Computer King
Statement of Owner's Equity
For Two Months Ended December 31, 1999

Pat King, capital, November 1, 1999		$ 0
Investment on November 1, 1999	$15,000	
Net income for November and December	7,205	
	$22,205	
Less withdrawals	4,000	
Increase in owner's equity		18,205
Pat King, capital, December 31, 1999		$18,205

Notes:

Computer King
Balance Sheet
December 31, 1999

ASSETS

Current assets:

Cash	$ 2,065	
Accounts receivable	2,720	
Supplies	760	
Prepaid insurance	2,300	
Total current assets		$ 7,845

Property, plant, and equipment:

Land	$10,000	
Office equipment	1,800	
Less accum. depr.	(50)	
Total property, plant, and equipment		11,750
Total assets		$19,595

LIABILITIES

Current liabilities:

Accounts payable	$ 900	
Wages payable	250	
Unearned rent	240	
Total liabilities		$ 1,390

OWNER'S EQUITY

Pat King, capital		18,205
Total liabilities and owner's equity		$19,595

Notes:

The Closing Process

Close Expenses

Close Revenues

Wages Expense
Bal. 4,525 | 4,525

Rent Expense
Bal. 1,600 | 1,600

Depreciation Expense
Bal. 50 | 50

Utilities Expense
Bal. 985 | 985

Supplies Expense
Bal. 2,040 | 2,040

Insurance Expense
Bal. 100 | 100

Miscellaneous Expense
Bal. 455 | 455

Income Summary

| 9,755 | 16,960 |
| Total Expenses | Total Revenues |

Pat King, Capital
Bal. 15,000

Pat King, Drawing
Bal. 4,000

Fees Earned
16,840 | Bal. 16,840

Rent Revenue
120 | Bal. 120

Record the journal entries to close the revenue accounts and the expense accounts.

Date	Description	Debit	Credit

The Closing Process

Close Income Summary

Income Summary	
9,755	16,960
7,205	
Closed	

Pat King, Capital	
	Bal. 15,000
	7,205
	Net Income

Close Drawing

Pat King, Drawing	
Bal. 4,000	4,000
Closed	

Pat King, Capital	
4,000	Bal. 15,000
Drawing	7,205
	Net Income

Record the journal entries to close the Income Summary
account and the Pat King, Drawing account

Date	Description	Debit	Credit

Notes:

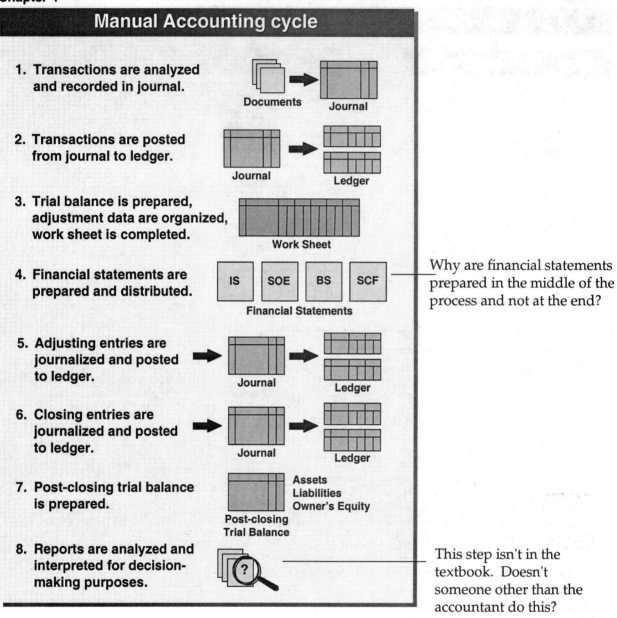

Manual Accounting cycle

1. **Transactions are analyzed and recorded in journal.**

Documents → Journal

2. **Transactions are posted from journal to ledger.**

Journal → Ledger

3. **Trial balance is prepared, adjustment data are organized, work sheet is completed.**

Work Sheet

4. **Financial statements are prepared and distributed.**

IS | SOE | BS | SCF

Financial Statements

Why are financial statements prepared in the middle of the process and not at the end?

5. **Adjusting entries are journalized and posted to ledger.**

Journal → Ledger

6. **Closing entries are journalized and posted to ledger.**

Journal → Ledger

7. **Post-closing trial balance is prepared.**

Assets
Liabilities
Owner's Equity

Post-closing Trial Balance

8. **Reports are analyzed and interpreted for decision-making purposes.**

This step isn't in the textbook. Doesn't someone other than the accountant do this?

Notes:

Chapter 4

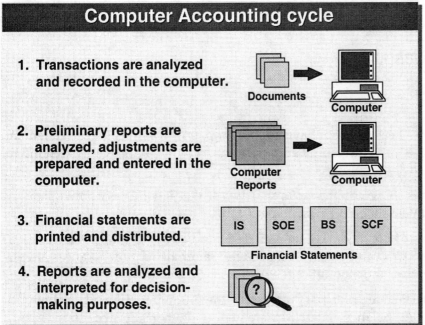

Computer Accounting cycle

1. Transactions are analyzed and recorded in the computer.

   Documents → Computer

2. Preliminary reports are analyzed, adjustments are prepared and entered in the computer.

   Computer Reports → Computer

3. Financial statements are printed and distributed.

   IS | SOE | BS | SCF
   Financial Statements

4. Reports are analyzed and interpreted for decision-making purposes.

Compare the computer accounting cycle with the manual cycle. Where are the major differences?

Financial Analysis and Interpretation

Working Capital and Current Ratio

Objective: Analyze and interpret the financial solvency of a business by computing the working capital and the current ratio.

Working Capital (WC)

Current Assets minus Current Liabilities

Current Ratio (CR)

$$\frac{\text{Current Assets}}{\text{Current Liabilities}}$$

Example

Computer King

WC = $7,845 - $1,390 = $6,455

CR = $7,845 / $1,390 = 5.6

True / False Questions

1. If the work sheet does not have a separate pair of columns for the statement of owner's equity, the capital and drawing account balances are extended to the Balance Sheet columns.

2. A net loss is shown on the work sheet in the credit columns of both the Income Statement columns and the Balance Sheet columns.

3. If the totals of the Income Statement debit and credit columns of a work sheet are $22,750 and $25,000, respectively, after all account balances have been extended, the amount of the net loss is $2,250.

4. The financial statements are prepared in the following order: (1) Income Statement, (2) Balance Sheet, (3) Statement of Owner's Equity.

5. On the income statement, miscellaneous expenses are usually presented as the last item without regard for the dollar amount.

6. The difference between a classified balance sheet and one that is not classified is that the classified one cannot be shown to individuals outside the company.

7. Cash and other assets that may reasonably be expected to be realized in cash, sold, or consumed through the normal operations of a business, usually within one year or less, are called current assets.

8. Fixed assets are also known as current assets.

9. Depreciation Expense is a permanent owner's equity account.

10. The amount of the net income for a period appears on both the income statement and the statement of owner's equity for that period.

11. Prepaid expenses that benefit a relatively short period of time are listed on the balance sheet as current liabilities.

12. The term "unearned" in the name of an account indicates the account represents a liability.

13. Since the adjustments are recorded on the work sheet, it is not necessary to post them in the ledger.

14. A period ending when an entity's activities have reached the lowest point in the annual operating cycle is termed the fiscal year.

Instructions:

Place a check mark in the appropriate column.

Multiple Choice Questions

____ 1. Net income appears on the work sheet in the:
   a. debit column of the Balance Sheet columns
   b. debit column of the Adjustments columns
   c. debit column of the Income Statement columns
   d. credit column of the Income Statement columns

____ 2. Which of the following appears in the Balance Sheet columns of the work sheet?
   a. Unearned Fees   b. Earned Revenue
   c. Depreciation Expense   d. Service Revenue

____ 3. After all of the account balances have been extended to the Balance Sheet columns of the work sheet, the totals of the Debit and Credit columns are $30,750 and $21,750, respectively. What is the amount of net income or net loss for the period?
   a. $9,000 net income   b. $9,000 net loss
   c. $30,750 net income   d. $52,400 net income

____ 4. When preparing the statement of owner's equity, the beginning capital balance can always be found:
   a. in the Income Statement columns of the work sheet
   b. by subtracting expenses from revenue
   c. in the general ledger
   d. in the general journal

____ 5. Accumulated Depreciation appears on the:
   a. Balance Sheet in the Current Assets section
   b. Balance Sheet in the Property, plant, and equipment section
   c. Balance Sheet in the Long-Term Liabilities section
   d. Income Statement as an Operating Expense

____ 6. Which one of the fixed asset accounts listed below will not have a related contra asset account?
   a. Office Equipment b. Land c. Delivery Equipment d. Building

____ 7. The cost of office supplies to be used in future periods is ordinarily shown on the balance sheet as a:
   a. plant asset b. current asset c. contra asset d. current liability

____ 8. Which of the following accounts will NOT be closed to Income Summary at the end of the fiscal year?
   a. Salaries Expense b. Fees Earned c. Drawing d. Depreciation Expense

Instructions:

Enter the letter of the best answer in the space provided.

Power Notes

Learning Objectives

1. **Basic Accounting Systems**
2. **Internal Control**
3. **Manual Accounting Systems**
4. **Adapting Manual Accounting Systems**
5. **Computerized Accounting Systems**

Power Note Topics

- **Internal Control Framework, Procedures**
- **Special Journals, Ledgers**
- **Revenue Journal and Ledgers**
- **Cash Receipts Journal and Ledgers**
- **Purchases Journal and Ledgers**
- **Cash Payments Journal and Ledgers**

Notes:

Internal Control Framework

1. Control Environment
2. Risk Assessment
3. Control Procedures
4. Monitoring
5. Information and Communication

Communication
Monitoring
Control Procedures
Risk Assessment
Control Environment

Internal Control Procedures

- Competent Personnel
- Rotating Duties
- Assigning Responsibility
- Separating Responsibilities for Related Operations
- Separating Accounting and Asset Custody
- Proofs and Security Measures

Special Journals

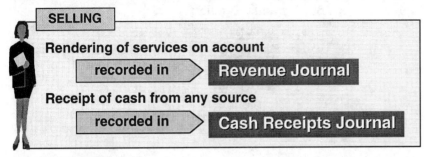

SELLING

Rendering of services on account

recorded in > **Revenue Journal**

Receipt of cash from any source

recorded in > **Cash Receipts Journal**

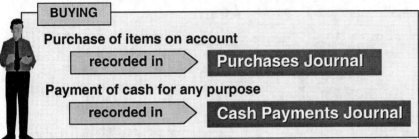

BUYING

Purchase of items on account

recorded in > **Purchases Journal**

Payment of cash for any purpose

recorded in > **Cash Payments Journal**

General Ledger and Subsidiary Ledgers

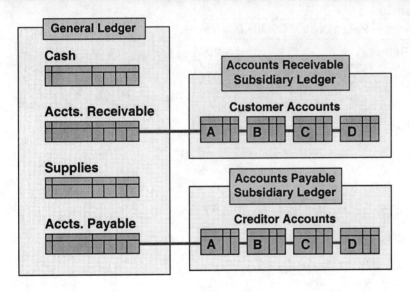

Notes:

Revenue Journal				Page 35
Date	Invoice No.	Account Debited	Post Ref.	Accts. Rec. – Debit Fees Earned – Credit
3/2	615	Handler Co.	✓	2,200
3/6	616	Jordan Co.	✓	1,750
3/18	617	Kenner Co.	✓	2,650
3/27	618	Handler Co.	✓	3,000
		Totals		9,600
				(12) (41)

Posting from the Revenue Journal to the Accounts Receivable Subsidiary Ledger

Accounts Receivable Subsidiary Ledger

Handler Co.

Date	Item	P.R.	Debit	Credit	Balance
3/2		R35	2,200		2,200
3/27		R35	3,000		5,200

Jordan Co.

Date	Item	P.R.	Debit	Credit	Balance
3/6		R35	1,750		1,750

Kenner Co.

Date	Item	P.R.	Debit	Credit	Balance
3/1	Bal.	✓			3,400
3/18		R35	2,650		6,050

Can these postings be made during the month?

Notes:

Revenue Journal

Page 35

Date	Invoice No.	Account Debited	Post Ref.	Accts. Rec. – Debit Fees Earned – Credit
3/2	615	Handler Co.	✓	2,200
3/6	616	Jordan Co.	✓	1,750
3/18	617	Kenner Co.	✓	2,650
3/27	618	Handler Co.	✓	3,000
		Totals		9,600
				(12) (41)

General Ledger

Posting from the Revenue Journal to the General Ledger

Account: Accounts Receivable					No. 12
Date	Item	P.R.	Debit	Credit	Balance
3/1	Bal.	✓			3,400
3/31		R35	9,600		13,000

Account: Fees Earned					No. 41
Date	Item	P.R.	Debit	Credit	Balance
3/31		R35		9,600	9,600

Notes:

Cash Receipts Journal · Page 14

Date	Account Credited	Post Ref.	Other Accounts Credit	Accounts Receivable Credit	Cash Debit
3/1	Rent Revenue	42	400		400
3/19	Kenner Co.	✓		3,400	3,400
3/28	Handler Co.	✓		2,200	2,200
3/30	Jordan Co.	✓		1,750	1,750
	Totals		400	7,350	7,750
			(✓)	(12)	(11)

Posting from the Cash Receipts Journal to the Accounts Receivable Subsidiary Ledger

Accounts Receivable Subsidiary Ledger

Handler Co.

Date	Item	P.R.	Debit	Credit	Balance
3/2		R35	2,200		2,200
3/27		R35	3,000		5,200
3/28		CR14		2,200	3,000

Jordan Co.

Date	Item	P.R.	Debit	Credit	Balance
3/6		R35	1,750		1,750
3/30		CR14		1,750	0

Kenner Co.

Date	Item	P.R.	Debit	Credit	Balance
3/1	Bal.	✓			3,400
3/18		R35	2,650		6,050
3/19		CR14		3,400	2,650

Notes:

Cash Receipts Journal — Page 14

Date	Account Credited	Post Ref.	Other Accounts Credit	Accounts Receivable Credit	Cash Debit
3/1	Rent Revenue	42	400		400
3/19	Kenner Co.	✓		3,400	3,400
3/28	Handler Co.	✓		2,200	2,200
3/30	Jordan Co.	✓		1,750	1,750
	Totals		400	7,350	7,750
			(✓)	(12)	(11)

General Ledger

Posting from the Cash Receipts Journal to the General Ledger

Account: Cash — No. 11

Date	Item	P.R.	Debit	Credit	Balance
3/1	Bal.	✓			6,200
3/31		CR14	7,750		13,950

Account: Accounts Receivable — No. 12

Date	Item	P.R.	Debit	Credit	Balance
3/1	Bal.	✓			3,400
3/31		R35	9,600		13,000
3/31		CR14		7,350	5,650

Account: Rent Revenue — No. 42

Date	Item	P.R.	Debit	Credit	Balance
3/1		CR14		400	400

Notes:

General Ledger

Account: Accounts Receivable					No. 12
Date	Item	P.R.	Debit	Credit	Balance
3/1	Bal.	✓			3,400
3/31		R35	9,600		13,000
3/31		CR14		7,350	5,650

Accounts Receivable Control Account

Accounts Receivable Subsidiary Ledger

Handler Co.					
Date	Item	P.R.	Debit	Credit	Balance
3/2		R35	2,200		2,200
3/27		R35	3,000		5,200
3/28		CR14		2,200	3,000

Jordan Co.					
Date	Item	P.R.	Debit	Credit	Balance
3/6		R35	1,750		1,750
3/30		CR14		1,750	0

Kenner Co.					
Date	Item	P.R.	Debit	Credit	Balance
3/1	Bal.	✓			3,400
3/18		R35	2,650		6,050
3/19		CR14		3,400	2,650

Purchases Journal   Page 11

Date	Account Credited	Post Ref.	Accts Payable Credit	Supplies Debit	Other Accounts Debit	Post Ref.	Amount
3/3	Howard Supplies	✓	600	600			
3/7	Donnelly Supplies	✓	420	420			
3/12	Jewett Bus. Syst.	✓	2,800		Office Equip. 18		2,800
3/19	Donnelly Supplies	✓	1,450	1,450			
3/27	Howard Supplies	✓	960	960			
	Totals		6,230	3,430			2,800
			(21)	(14)			(✓)

Posting from the Purchases Journal to the Accounts Payable Subsidiary Ledger

Accounts Payable Subsidiary Ledger

Donnelly Supplies

Date	Item	P.R.	Debit	Credit	Balance
3/7		P11		420	420
3/19		P11		1,450	1,870

Grayco Supplies

Date	Item	P.R.	Debit	Credit	Balance
3/1	Bal.	✓			1,230

Howard Supplies

Date	Item	P.R.	Debit	Credit	Balance
3/3		P11		600	600
3/27		P11		960	1,560

Jewett Business Systems

Date	Item	P.R.	Debit	Credit	Balance
3/12		P11		2,800	2,800

Notes:

Purchases Journal							Page 11
Date	Account Credited	Post Ref.	Accts Payable Credit	Supplies Debit	Other Accounts Debit	Post Ref.	Amount
3/3	Howard Supplies	✓	600	600			
3/7	Donnelly Supplies	✓	420	420			
3/12	Jewett Bus. Syst.	✓	2,800		Office Equip.	18	2,800
3/19	Donnelly Supplies	✓	1,450	1,450			
3/27	Howard Supplies	✓	960	960			
	Totals		6,230	3,430			2,800
			(21)	(14)			(✓)

General Ledger

Posting from the Purchases Journal to the General Ledger

Account: Accounts Payable					No. 21
Date	Item	P.R.	Debit	Credit	Balance
3/1	Bal.	✓			1,230
3/31		P11		6,230	7,460

Account: Supplies					No. 14
Date	Item	P.R.	Debit	Credit	Balance
3/1	Bal.	✓			2,500
3/31		P11	3,430		5,930

Account: Office Equipment					No. 18
Date	Item	P.R.	Debit	Credit	Balance
3/1	Bal.	✓			2,500
3/12		P11	2,800		5,300

Notes:

Chapter 5

Cash Payments Journal — Page 7

Date	Ck. No.	Account Debited	Post Ref.	Other Accounts Debit	Accounts Payable Debit	Cash Credit
3/2	150	Rent Expense	52	1,600		1,600
3/15	151	Grayco Supplies	✓		1,230	1,230
3/21	152	Jewett Bus. Syst.	✓		2,800	2,800
3/22	153	Donnelly Supplies	✓		420	420
3/30	154	Utilities Expense	54	1,050		1,050
3/31	155	Howard Supplies	✓		600	600
		Totals		2,650	5,050	7,700
				(✓)	(21)	(11)

Accounts Payable Subsidiary Ledger

Posting from the Cash Payments Journal to the Accounts Payable Subsidiary Ledger

Donnelly Supplies

Date	Item	P.R.	Debit	Credit	Balance
3/7		P11		420	420
3/19		P11		1,450	1,870
3/22		CP7	420		1,450

Grayco Supplies

Date	Item	P.R.	Debit	Credit	Balance
3/1	Bal.	✓			1,230
3/15		CP7	1,230		0

Howard Supplies

Date	Item	P.R.	Debit	Credit	Balance
3/3		P11		600	600
3/27		P11		960	1,560
3/31		CP7	600		960

Jewett Business Systems

Date	Item	P.R.	Debit	Credit	Balance
3/12		P11		2,800	2,800
3/21		CP7	2,800		0

Cash Payments Journal — Page 7

Date	Ck. No.	Account Debited	Post Ref.	Other Accounts Debit	Accounts Payable Debit	Cash Credit
3/2	150	Rent Expense	52	1,600		1,600
3/15	151	Grayco Supplies	✓		1,230	1,230
3/21	152	Jewett Bus. Syst.	✓		2,800	2,800
3/22	153	Donnelly Supp.	✓		420	420
3/30	154	Utilities Expense	54	1,050		1,050
3/31	155	Howard Supplies	✓		600	600
		Totals		2,650	5,050	7,700
				(✓)	(21)	(11)

General Ledger

Posting from the Cash Payments Journal to the General Ledger

Account: Accounts Payable — No. 21

Date	Item	P.R.	Debit	Credit	Balance
3/1	Bal.	✓			1,230
3/31		P11		6,230	7,460
3/31		CP7	5,050		2,410

Account: Cash — No. 11

Date	Item	P.R.	Debit	Credit	Balance
3/1	Bal.	✓			6,200
3/31		CR14	7,750		13,950
3/31		CP7		7,700	6,250

Account: Rent Expense — No. 52

Date	Item	P.R.	Debit	Credit	Balance
3/2		CP7	1,600		1,600

Account: Utilities Expense — No. 54

Date	Item	P.R.	Debit	Credit	Balance
3/30		CP7	1,050		1,050

When are these postings made?

General Ledger

Account: Accounts Payable					No. 21	Accounts Payable Control Account
Date	Item	P.R.	Debit	Credit	Balance	
3/1	Bal.	✓			1,230	
3/31		P11		6,230	7,460	
3/31		CP7	5,050		**2,410**	

Accounts Payable Subsidiary Ledger

Donnelly Supplies

Date	Item	P.R.	Debit	Credit	Balance
3/7		P11		420	420
3/19		P11		1,450	1,870
3/22		CP7	420		**1,450**

Grayco Supplies

Date	Item	P.R.	Debit	Credit	Balance
3/1	Bal.	✓			1,230
3/15		CP7	1,230		**0**

Howard Supplies

Date	Item	P.R.	Debit	Credit	Balance
3/3		P11		600	600
3/27		P11		960	1,560
3/31		CP7	600		**960**

Jewett Business Systems

Date	Item	P.R.	Debit	Credit	Balance
3/12		P11		2,800	2,800
3/21		CP7	2,800		**0**

True / False Questions

True   False

_____ _____   1. System analysis is the final phase of the creation or revision of an accounting system and is concerned with implementing proposals.

_____ _____   2. The control environment is affected by what is actually practiced rather than by the written procedure if the two are different.

_____ _____   3. Adherence to good internal controls would require the hiring of competent employees and then rotating them from job to job.

_____ _____   4. Good internal control requires that one employee handle the tasks of ordering supplies, receiving the supplies, and paying the supplier.

_____ _____   5. Entries to correct errors are recorded in the general journal.

_____ _____   6. The total of the amount column in the revenue journal is posted as a debit to Accounts Receivable and a credit to Fees Earned.

_____ _____   7. The purchase of supplies for cash would be recorded in the purchases journal.

_____ _____   8. The customers ledger and the creditors ledger refer to subsidiary ledgers.

_____ _____   9. A cash refund paid to a customer who overpaid an account receivable is recorded in the cash payments journal.

_____ _____   10. Sales of office supplies for cash to a neighboring business, as an accommodation, are recorded in the revenue journal.

_____ _____   11. For some companies it is prudent to have subsidiary ledgers for equipment.

_____ _____   12. When a special journal is used, the amount columns should not be totaled before posting to the ledger at the end of the accounting period.

Instructions:

Place a check mark in the appropriate column.

Multiple Choice Questions

____ 1. Broad principles that apply to all accounting systems include:
a. adaptability to future needs and materiality
b. separate entity and adequate net assets
c. adherence to the net worth theory and internal controls
d. cost-benefit balance and effective reports

____ 2. To determine information needs, the sources of such information, and the deficiencies in procedures and data processing methods presently used is the goal of:
a. systems design   b. accounting systems
c. systems analysis   d. internal auditing

____ 3. The three phases of setting up an accounting system are, in order:
a. design, implementation, analysis
b. analysis, design, implementation
c. design, analysis, implementation
d. implementation, design, analysis

____ 4. An element of internal control is:
a. risk assessment   b. journals
c. subsidiary ledgers   d. controlling accounts

____ 5. Every controlling account must have its own:
a. revenue ledger   b. general ledger
c. subsidiary ledger   d. journal

____ 6. The controlling account in the general ledger that summarizes the debits and credits to the individual customer accounts in the subsidiary ledger is entitled:
a. Purchases   b. Accounts Payable
c. Fees Earned   d. Accounts Receivable

____ 7. Which of the following is recorded in the cash payments journal?
a. adjusting entry for accrued salaries
b. receipt of cash on supplies returned
c. receipt of cash from services rendered
d. payment of employees' salaries

____ 8. In which journal is the receipt of a note from a customer on account recorded?
a. revenue journal   b. cash receipts journal
c. general journal   d. purchases journal

Instructions:

Enter the letter of the best answer in the space provided.

Learning Objectives

1. Nature of Merchandising Business
2a. Accounting for Purchases
2b. Accounting for Sales
2c. Transportation Costs
2d. Merchandise Transactions
3. Merchandising Chart of Accounts
4. Merchandising Income Statement
5. Merchandising Accounting Cycle
6. Financial Analysis and Interpretation

C6

Power Note Topics

- Nature of Merchandising Businesses
- Inventory Costs and Relationships
- Perpetual Inventory Systems
- Merchandising Transactions
- Merchandising Chart of Accounts
- Merchandising Financial Statements
- Ratio of Net Sales to Assets

Notes:

Income Statement Comparison

Service Business

Fees earned	$150,000
Operating expenses	120,000
Net income	$ 30,000

20% of revenues

How do I calculate these percentages?

Merchandising Business

Sales revenue	$600,000
Cost of mdse. sold	450,000
Gross profit	$150,000
Operating expenses	120,000
Net income	$ 30,000

75% of revenues

5% of revenues

Inventory Costs and Relationships

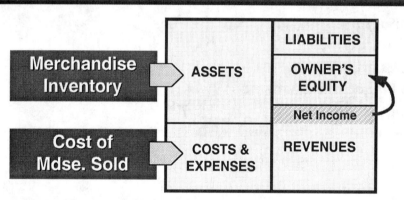

If merchandise inventory is . . . . overstated

Cost of merchandise sold is . . . . . .

Gross profit and net income are . . .

Ending owner's equity is . . . .

How would an error in determining ending merchandise inventory affect profitability?

If merchandise inventory is . . . . understated

Cost of merchandise sold is . . . . . .

Gross profit and net income are . . .

Ending owner's equity is . . . .

Merchandising and Inventory

- ✔ **Merchandising involves selling inventory**
- ✔ **Inventory is usually an important asset**
- ✔ **Inventory must be accounted for <u>periodically</u> or <u>perpetually</u>**
- ✔ **Traditional periodic method is often being replaced by <u>perpetual</u> inventory accounting**

Advantages of Using Perpetual Inventory

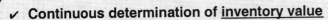
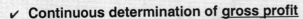
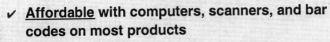

- ✔ **Continuous determination of <u>inventory value</u>**
- ✔ **Continuous determination of <u>gross profit</u>**
- ✔ **<u>Affordable</u> with computers, scanners, and bar codes on most products**
- ✔ **Perpetual inventory accounting provides management <u>controls</u>**
- ✔ **Managers know which items are selling fastest and the profit margin on those items**

Notes:

Perpetual Inventory System

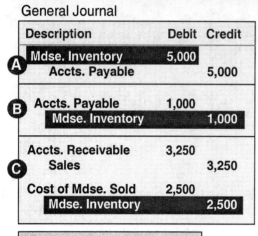

General Journal

Description	Debit	Credit
Ⓐ Mdse. Inventory	5,000	
Accts. Payable		5,000
Ⓑ Accts. Payable	1,000	
Mdse. Inventory		1,000
Ⓒ Accts. Receivable	3,250	
Sales		3,250
Cost of Mdse. Sold	2,500	
Mdse. Inventory		2,500

General Ledger

Mdse. Inventory

Ⓐ 5,000	1,000 Ⓑ
	2,500 Ⓒ

Bal 1,500

Cost of Mdse. Sold

Ⓒ 2,500

Ⓐ Purchase on account
Ⓑ Return of merchandise
Ⓒ Sale of merchandise

In a **perpetual system**, Mdse. Inventory is an active asset account. All changes are recorded as they occur.

Credit Terms, Cash Discounts

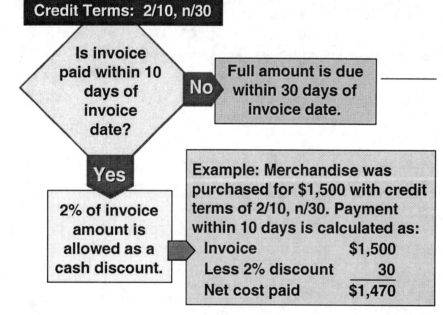

Credit Terms: 2/10, n/30

Is invoice paid within 10 days of invoice date?

No → Full amount is due within 30 days of invoice date.

Yes → 2% of invoice amount is allowed as a cash discount.

Example: Merchandise was purchased for $1,500 with credit terms of 2/10, n/30. Payment within 10 days is calculated as:

Invoice	$1,500
Less 2% discount	30
Net cost paid	$1,470

Do some companies take the discount even if the payment is past the discount period allowed?

Selling and Buying Merchandise Inventory

Seller

Description	Debit	Credit
Accts. Receivable	1,500	
Sales		1,500
Cost of Mdse. Sold	900	
Mdse. Inventory		900

Jan 12. Merchandise was sold with credit terms of 2/10, n/30.

Description	Debit	Credit
Cash	1,470	
Sales Discounts	30	
Accts. Receivable		1,500

Jan 22. Payment was made within the discount period.

Buyer

Description	Debit	Credit
Mdse. Inventory	1,470	
Accts. Payable		1,470

Recorded at net cost $1,500 - $30 (discount)

Why would a company record this net of cost?

Description	Debit	Credit
Accts. Payable	1,470	
Cash		1,470

How would this be recorded if payment was not made in the discount period?

Seller

Description	Debit	Credit
Accts. Receivable	1,500	
Sales		1,500
Cost of Mdse. Sold	900	
Mdse. Inventory		900

Jan 12. Merchandise was sold with credit terms of 2/10, n/30.

Description	Debit	Credit
Cash	1,470	
Sales Discounts	30	
Accts. Receivable		1,500

Jan 22. Payment was made within the discount period.

Buyer

Description	Debit	Credit
Mdse. Inventory	1,500	
Accts. Payable		1,500

Recorded at full cost

Is it better to always record the purchase at cost?

Description	Debit	Credit
Accts. Payable	1,500	
Mdse. Inventory		30
Cash		1,470

How would this be recorded if payment was not made in the discount period?

Notes:

Computer King
Merchandising Chart of Accounts
Balance Sheet Accounts

100 Assets
110 Cash
111 Notes Receivable
112 Accounts Receivable
113 Interest Receivable
115 Merchandise Inventory
116 Office Supplies
117 Prepaid Insurance
120 Land
123 Store Equipment
124 Accumulated Depreciation—
　　Store Equipment
125 Office Equipment
126 Accumulated Depreciation—
　　Office Equipment

200 Liabilities
210 Accounts Payable
211 Salaries Payable
212 Unearned Rent
215 Notes Payable

300 Owner's Equity
310 Pat King, Capital
311 Pat King, Drawing
312 Income Summary

Income Statement Accounts

400 Revenues
410 Sales
411 Sales Returns and Allowances
412 Sales Discounts

600 Other Income
610 Rent Revenue
611 Interest Revenue

700 Other Expense
710 Interest Expense

500 Costs and Expenses
510 Cost of Merchandise Sold
520 Sales Salaries Expense
521 Advertising Expense
522 Depreciation Expense—
　　Store Equipment
523 Transportation Out
529 Misc. Selling Expense
530 Office Salaries Expense
531 Rent Expense
532 Depreciation Expense—
　　Office Equipment
533 Insurance Expense
534 Office Supplies Expense
539 Misc. Admin. Expense

Is this chart of accounts used with the periodic method or the perpetual method? How would they be different?

Notes:

Computer King
Income Statement (Multiple-Step)
For the Year Ended December 31, 2001

Revenue from sales:		
Sales		$ 720,185
Less:Sales returns and allow.	$ 6,140	
Sales discounts	5,790	11,930
Net sales		$708,255
Cost of merchandise sold		525,305
Gross profit		$182,950
Operating expenses:		
Selling expenses:		
Sales salaries expense	$60,030	
Advertising expense	10,860	
Depr. expense–store equip.	3,100	
Miscellaneous selling expense	630	
Total selling expenses		$ 74,620
Administrative expenses:		
Office salaries expense	$21,020	
Rent expense	8,100	
Depr. expense–office equip.	2,490	
Insurance expense	1,910	
Office supplies expense	610	
Misc. admin. expenses	760	
Total admin. expenses	34,890	
Total operating expenses		109,510
Income from operations		$ 73,440
Other income:		
Interest revenue	$3,800	
Rent revenue	600	
Total other income	$4,400	
Other expense:		
Interest expense	2,440	1,960
Net income		$75,400

How do I calculate percentages based on net sales?

Notes:

Computer King		
Income Statement (Single-Step)		
For the Year Ended December 31, 2001		

Revenues:

Net sales		$708,255
Interest revenue		3,800
Rent revenue		600
Total revenues		$712,655

Expenses:

Cost of merchandise sold	$525,305	
Selling expenses	74,620	
Administrative expenses	34,890	
Interest expense	2,440	
Total expenses		637,255
Net income		**$ 75,400**

What are the disadvantages of the single-step income statement? What are the advantages?

Notes:

Computer King
Balance Sheet
December 31, 2001

Assets

Current assets:		
Cash		$ 52,950
Notes receivable		40,000
Accounts receivable		60,880
Interest receivable		200
Merchandise inventory		62,150
Office supplies		480
Prepaid insurance		2,650
Total current assets		$219,310
Property, plant, and equipment:		
Land		$ 10,000
Store equipment	$ 27,100	
Less accum. depreciation	5,700	21,400
Office equipment	$ 15,570	
Less accum. depreciation	4,720	10,850
Total property, plant, and equipment		42,250
Total assets		$261,560

Liabilities

Current liabilities:		
Accounts payable	$ 22,420	
Note payable (current portion)	5,000	
Salaries payable	1,140	
Unearned rent	1,800	
Total current liabilities		$30,360
Long-term liabilities:		
Note payable (due 2004)		20,000
Total liabilities		$ 50,360

Owner's Equity

Pat King, capital	211,200
Total liabilities and owner's equity	$261,560

How do I calculate percentages based on total assets?

Notes:

True / False Questions

True   False

_____	_____	1.	On the income statement, operating expenses are subtracted from revenue for a service business and from gross profit for a merchandising business.
_____	_____	2.	Cost of merchandise sold is the same as operating expenses.
_____	_____	3.	A buyer who acquires merchandise under credit terms of 1/10, n/30 has 20 days after the invoice date to take advantage of the cash discount.
_____	_____	4.	In a perpetual inventory system, merchandise returned to vendors reduces the merchandise inventory account.
_____	_____	5.	Under a periodic inventory system, both the sales amount and the cost of merchandise sold amount are recorded when each item of merchandise is sold.
_____	_____	6.	Sales Discounts normally has a debit balance.
_____	_____	7.	A sale of $600 on account, subject to a sales tax of 5%, would be recorded as an account receivable of $600.
_____	_____	8.	If the ownership of merchandise passes to the buyer when the seller delivers the merchandise for shipment, the terms are stated as FOB destination.
_____	_____	9.	If merchandise costing $2,500, terms FOB destination, 2/10, n/30, with prepaid transportation costs of $100, is paid within 10 days, the amount of the purchases discount is $52.
_____	_____	10.	The chart of accounts for a merchandising business would include an account called Merchandise Inventory.
_____	_____	11.	On the multiple-step income statement, the total of all expenses is deducted from the total of all revenues.
_____	_____	12.	Selling expenses are divided into general and operating expenses.
_____	_____	13.	A criticism of the single-step income statement is that gross profit and income from operations are not readily available for analysis.
_____	_____	14.	The adjusting entry to record inventory shrinkage would include a debit to Merchandise Inventory.

Instructions:

Place a check mark in the appropriate column.

Multiple Choice Questions

____ 1. The difference between sales and cost of merchandise sold for a merchandising business is:
a. sales   b. net sales   c. gross sales   d. gross profit

____ 2. When purchases of merchandise are made for cash, the transaction may be recorded with the following entry:
a. debit Cash, credit Merchandise Inventory
b. debit Merchandise Inventory, credit Cash
c. debit Merchandise Inventory, credit Cash Discounts
d. debit Merchandise Inventory, credit Purchases

____ 3. When merchandise is purchased to resell to customers, it is recorded in the account entitled:
a. Supplies   b. Capital   c. Merchandise Inventory   d. Sales

____ 4. The amount of the total cash paid to the seller for merchandise purchased would normally include:
a. only the list price   b. only the sales tax
c. the list price plus the sales tax   d. the list price less the sales tax

____ 5. The inventory system employing accounting records that continuously disclose the amount of inventory is called:
a. retail   b. periodic   c. physical   d. perpetual

____ 6. Using a perpetual inventory system, the entry to record the sale of merchandise on account includes a:
a. debit to Sales   b. debit to Merchandise Inventory
c. credit to Merchandise Inventory   d. credit to Accounts Receivable

____ 7. If title to merchandise purchased passes to the buyer when the goods are delivered to the buyer, the terms are:
a. consigned   b. n/30   c. FOB shipping point   d. FOB destination

____ 8. When the three sections of a balance sheet are presented on a page in a downward sequence, it is called the:
a. account form   b. comparative form
c. horizontal form   d. report form

Instructions:

Enter the letter of the best answer in the space provided.

Power Notes

Learning Objectives

1. Cash and Cash Controls
2. Internal Control of Cash Receipts
3. Internal Control of Cash Payments
4. Bank Accounts: A Cash Control
5. Bank Reconciliation
6. Petty Cash
7. Balance Sheet Cash Presentation
8. Financial Analysis and Interpretation

C 7

Power Note Topics

- Cash Accounts and Internal Controls
- Cash Receipts and Controls
- Cash Payments and Controls
- Bank Reconciliation
- Petty Cash Accounting
- Ratio of Cash to Current Liabilities

Notes:

Cash Accounts and Internal Controls

✔ Many companies need several cash accounts to account for different cash categories and funds.

✔ Most companies have multiple bank accounts. The title for each bank account should be:

✔ **Cash in Bank – (Name of Bank)**

✔ <u>Preventive controls</u> protect cash from theft and misuse of cash.

✔ <u>Detective controls</u> are designed to detect theft or misuse of cash and are also preventive in nature.

Internal Control of Cash Receipts

Cash is normally received from two sources:

1. Over the counter from cash customers.
   Use of a <u>cash register</u> is an important control.

2. Received in the mail from credit customers.
   Cash is in the form of <u>checks</u>.

All cash is sent to the <u>Cashier's Department</u>.

An employee prepares a <u>bank deposit ticket</u> and makes a bank deposit.

The bank deposit record is sent to the <u>Accounting Department</u> where it is recorded.

Notes:

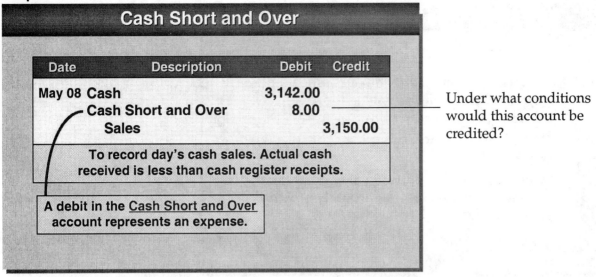

Cash Short and Over

Date	Description	Debit	Credit
May 08	Cash	3,142.00	
	Cash Short and Over	8.00	
	Sales		3,150.00
	To record day's cash sales. Actual cash received is less than cash register receipts.		

A debit in the <u>Cash Short and Over</u> account represents an expense.

Under what conditions would this account be credited?

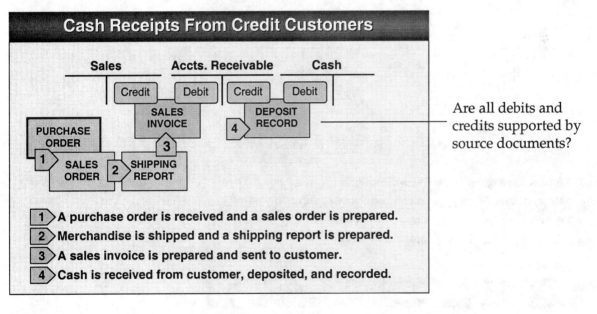

Cash Receipts From Credit Customers

1. A purchase order is received and a sales order is prepared.
2. Merchandise is shipped and a shipping report is prepared.
3. A sales invoice is prepared and sent to customer.
4. Cash is received from customer, deposited, and recorded.

Are all debits and credits supported by source documents?

Notes:

Internal Control of Cash Payments

1. Cash controls must provide assurance that payments are made for only <u>authorized</u> transactions.

2. Cash controls should ensure that cash is used <u>efficiently</u>.

3. A voucher system provides assurance that what is being paid for was properly <u>ordered</u>, <u>received</u>, and <u>billed</u> by the supplier.

Cash Payments to Suppliers

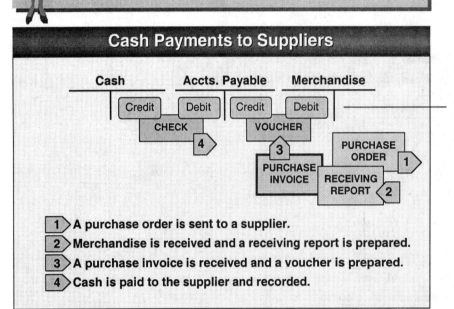

Are all debits and credits supported by source documents?

1 ⟩ A purchase order is sent to a supplier.
2 ⟩ Merchandise is received and a receiving report is prepared.
3 ⟩ A purchase invoice is received and a voucher is prepared.
4 ⟩ Cash is paid to the supplier and recorded.

Cash Receipts and Payments

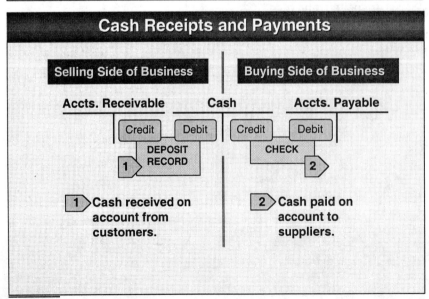

1 ⟩ Cash received on account from customers.

2 ⟩ Cash paid on account to suppliers.

Petty Cash Accounting

Date	Description	Debit	Credit
Aug. 1	Petty Cash	100.00	
	Cash		100.00
	To establish a petty cash fund.		
Aug. 31	Office Supplies	50.00	
	Store Supplies	35.00	
	Misc. Admin. Expense	3.00	
	Cash		88.00
	To replenish the petty cash fund.		

Are these credits supported by checks? If so, who is the payee?

Note: No entry in Petty Cash account when the fund is replenished.

Monroe Company
Bank Reconciliation
July 31, 2000

Balance per bank statement		$3,359.78
Add deposit in transit		816.20
		$4,175.98
Deduct outstanding checks:		
No. 812	$1,061.00	
No. 878	435.39	
No. 883	48.60	1,544.99
Adjusted balance		$2,630.99

Balance per depositor's records		$2,549.99
A Add note and interest collected by bank		408.00
		$2,957.99
B Deduct: Customer NSF check	$ 300.00	
Bank service charges	18.00	
Error in recording Ck. No. 879	9.00	327.00
Adjusted balance		$2,630.99

General Journal   Page 1

	Date	Description	P.R.	Debit	Credit
A	7/31	Cash	11	408.00	
		Notes Receivable			400.00
		Interest Revenue			8.00
B	7/31	Accts. Receivable - T. Ivey		300.00	
		Miscellaneous Expense		18.00	
		Accts. Payable - Taylor Co.		9.00	
		Cash	11		327.00

Could these two entries be combined into a single entry?

Bank Reconciliation - Journal and Ledger

General Journal   Page 1

Date	Description	P.R.	Debit	Credit
7/31	Cash	11	408.00	
	Notes Receivable			400.00
	Interest Revenue			8.00
7/31	Accts. Receivable - T. Ivey		300.00	
	Miscellaneous Expense		18.00	
	Accts. Payable - Taylor Co.		9.00	
	Cash	11		327.00

A (next to first 7/31 entry)

B (next to second 7/31 entry)

General Ledger

Account: Cash					Account No. 11	
					Balance	
Date	Item	P.R.	Debit	Credit	Debit	Credit
7/31	Balance				2,549.99	
7/31		J1	408.00		2,957.99	
7/31		J1		327.00	2,630.99	

Does this amount agree with the adjusted balance on the bank reconciliation?

Notes:

Solvency Analysis

Solvency is the ability of a business to meet its financial obligations (debts) as they are due.

Solvency analysis focuses on the ability of a business to pay or otherwise satisfy its current and noncurrent liabilities.

This ability is normally assessed by examining balance sheet relationships.

Solvency Measures — The Short-Term Creditor

Doomsday Ratio

	Laettner Co.	Oakley Co.
A. Cash and equivalents	$100,000	$ 120,000
B. Current liabilities	400,000	1,500,000
Doomsday ratio A / B	0.25	0.08

Use: To indicate the worst case assumption that should the business cease to exist, only the cash on hand is available to meet creditor obligations.

Notes:

True / False Questions

True   False

_____ _____ 1. A customer's check received in settlement of an account receivable is considered to be cash.

_____ _____ 2. If the balance in Cash Short and Over at the end of a period is a credit, it indicates that cash shortages have exceeded cash overages for the period.

_____ _____ 3. A voucher is a form on which is recorded pertinent data about a liability and the particulars of its payment.

_____ _____ 4. When the petty cash fund is replenished, the petty cash account is credited for the total of all expenditures made since the fund was last replenished.

_____ _____ 5. The party signing a check is called the payee.

_____ _____ 6. In preparing a bank reconciliation, the amount of outstanding checks is added to the balance per bank statement.

_____ _____ 7. The amount of the "adjusted balance" appearing on the bank reconciliation as of a given date is the amount that is shown on the balance sheet for that date.

_____ _____ 8. A debit memo from the bank indicates that the bank has deducted an amount from the depositor's account.

_____ _____ 9. In preparing a bank reconciliation, the amount indicated by a debit memorandum for bank service charges is deducted from the balance per depositor's records.

_____ _____ 10. Money market accounts, commercial paper, and United States Treasury Bills are examples of cash equivalents.

_____ _____ 11. The data needed to prepare entries based on the bank reconciliation are shown as adjustments to the balance per bank statement.

_____ _____ 12. A payment system that uses computerized electronic impulses to effect a cash transaction is called electronic funds transfer (EFT).

Instructions:

Place a check mark in the appropriate column.

Multiple Choice Questions

_____ 1. The notification accompanying a check that indicates the specific invoice being paid is called:
   a. voucher
   b. debit memorandum
   c. remittance advice
   d. credit memorandum

_____ 2. The debit balance in Cash Short and Over at the end of an accounting period is reported as:
   a. an expense on the income statement
   b. income on the income statement
   c. an asset on the balance sheet
   d. a liability on the balance sheet

_____ 3. An example of a preventive control is:
   a. the use of a bank account
   b. separating the Cashier Department and Accounting Department personnel
   c. bonding employees who handle cash
   d. accepting payment in currency only

_____ 4. The type of account and normal balance of Petty Cash is a(n):
   a. revenue, credit
   b. asset, debit
   c. liability, credit
   d. expense, debit

_____ 5. The debit recorded in the journal to establish the petty cash fund is to:
   a. Cash
   b. Petty Cash
   c. Accounts Receivable
   d. Accounts Payable

_____ 6. Journal entries based on the bank reconciliation are required in the depositor's accounts for:
   a. outstanding checks
   b. deposits in transit
   c. bank errors
   d. book errors

_____ 7. Cash equivalents:
   a. are illegal in some states
   b. will be converted to cash within two years
   c. will be converted to cash within 90 days
   d. are only available to large companies

Instructions:

Enter the letter of the best answer in the space provided.

Power Notes

Learning Objectives

1. Classification of Receivables
2. Internal Control of Receivables
3. Uncollectible Receivables
4. Uncollectibles – Allowance Method
5. Uncollectibles – Direct Write-Off Method
6. Characteristics of Notes Receivable
7. Accounting for Notes Receivable
8. Balance Sheet Presentation
9. Financial Analysis and Interpretation

C8

Power Note Topics

- Receivables – Classification and Control
- Uncollectibles – Direct Write-Off Method
- Uncollectibles –Allowance Method
- Accounting for Notes Receivable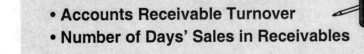
- Balance Sheet Presentation
- Accounts Receivable Turnover
- Number of Days' Sales in Receivables

Notes:

Classification of Receivables

✔ <u>Accounts Receivable</u> – used for selling merchandise or services on credit, and normally expected to be collected in a relatively short period.

✔ <u>Notes Receivable</u> – used to grant credit on the basis of a formal instrument of credit, called a promissory note.

✔ <u>Other Receivables</u> – interest receivable, taxes receivable, and receivables from officers or employees.

Why do companies loan money to officers and employees?

Notes:

Accounting for Uncollectible Accounts Receivable

The Direct Write-Off Method

- This method is not consistent with the matching principle. ——— Why not?

- Accounts that prove to be uncollectible are written off in the year they become worthless.

  How do we know when an account becomes worthless?

- Uncollectible Accounts Expense is debited and Accounts Receivable is credited for each such transaction.

Journal Entries – Direct Write-Off Method

Date	Description	Debit	Credit
May. 10	Uncollectible Accts. Expense	420	
	Accts. Receivable - D. L. Ross		420
	Write off uncollectible account of $420.		
Nov. 21	Accts. Receivable - D. L. Ross	420	
	Uncollectible Accts. Expense		420
	Cash	420	
	Accts. Receivable - D. L. Ross		420
	Reinstate and collect prior account written off.		

How does this entry affect net income?

Notes:

Accounting for Uncollectible Accounts Receivable

The Allowance Method

- This method is consistent with the matching principle.
- Management makes an estimate each year of the portion of accounts receivable that may not be collectible.
- Uncollectible Accounts Expense is debited and Allowance for Doubtful Accounts is credited.
- Actual accounts that prove to be uncollectible are debited to Allowance for Doubtful Accounts and credited to Accounts Receivable.

Why is it consistent with the matching principle?

Journal Entries – Allowance Method

Date	Description	Debit	Credit
Dec. 31	Uncollectible Accts. Expense	4,000	
	Allowance for Doubtful Acct.		4,000

Estimated a total of $4,000 will be uncollectible.

Date	Description	Debit	Credit
Jan. 21	Allowance for Doubtful Accts.	610	
	Accts. Receivable - J. Parker		610

Write off uncollectible account of $610.

Does this entry affect net income?

Date	Description	Debit	Credit
June 10	Accts. Receivable - J. Parker	610	
	Allowance for Doubtful Accts.		610
	Cash	610	
	Accts. Receivable - J. Parker		610

Reinstate and collect prior account written off.

Notes:

Estimating Uncollectible Accounts Expense

The allowance method uses two ways to estimate the amount debited to **Uncollectible Accounts Expense**.

1. <u>Estimate based on a percentage of sales.</u>

   If credit sales for the period are $300,000 and it is estimated that 1% will be uncollectible, the **Uncollectible Accounts Expense** is $3,000.

2. <u>Estimate based on analysis of receivables.</u>

   If it is estimated that $3,390 of the receivables will be uncollectible and the Allowance for Uncollectible Accounts is $510, the **Uncollectible Accounts Expense** is $2,880 ($3,390 – $510).

Practice:

Credit sales are $600,000 and we estimate that 1.5% will be uncollectible. How much is the Uncollectible Accounts Expense?

The Accounts Receivable balance is $2,400,000 and the Allowance for Uncollectible Accounts has a credit balance of $20,000. We estimate that $135,000 of the receivables will be uncollectible. How much is the Uncollectible Accounts Expense?

Accounts Receivable Aging and Uncollectibles

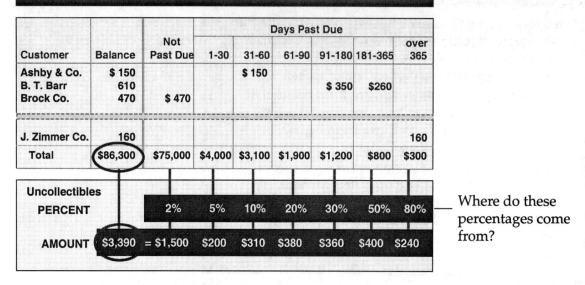

Customer	Balance	Not Past Due	Days Past Due					
			1-30	31-60	61-90	91-180	181-365	over 365
Ashby & Co.	$ 150			$ 150				
B. T. Barr	610					$ 350	$260	
Brock Co.	470	$ 470						
J. Zimmer Co.	160							160
Total	$86,300	$75,000	$4,000	$3,100	$1,900	$1,200	$800	$300

Uncollectibles

PERCENT		2%	5%	10%	20%	30%	50%	80%
AMOUNT	$3,390	= $1,500	$200	$310	$380	$360	$400	$240

Where do these percentages come from?

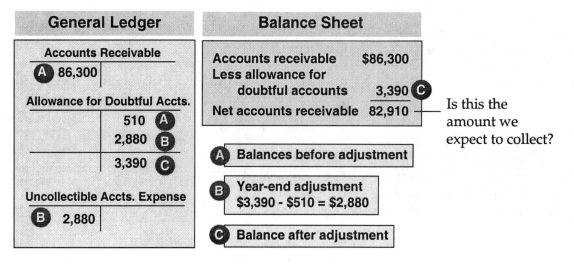

General Ledger

Accounts Receivable

Ⓐ 86,300

Allowance for Doubtful Accts.

	510 Ⓐ
	2,880 Ⓑ
	3,390 Ⓒ

Uncollectible Accts. Expense

Ⓑ 2,880

Balance Sheet

Accounts receivable $86,300
Less allowance for
    doubtful accounts   3,390 Ⓒ
Net accounts receivable   82,910

Is this the amount we expect to collect?

Ⓐ **Balances before adjustment**

Ⓑ **Year-end adjustment**
$3,390 - $510 = $2,880

Ⓒ **Balance after adjustment**

Notes:

Characteristics of Notes Receivable

A promissory note is a written document containing a promise to pay:

- ✓ a specific amount of money (principal)
- ✓ to a specific person or company (payee)
- ✓ at a specific place
- ✓ on a specific date or upon demand
- ✓ plus interest at a specific percentage of the principal (face) amount per year

Calculating Interest and Maturity Value

We received a $2,500, 10%, 90-day note dated March 16, 2000. —— What is the due date of this note?

Interest Calculation

Principal x Rate x Time = Interest

$2,500 x 10% x 90 /360 = $62.50

Maturity Value Calculation

Principal + Interest = Maturity Value

$2,500 + $62.50 = $2,562.50

Notes:

Accounting for Notes Receivable

Date	Description	Debit	Credit
Nov. 21	Notes Receivable	6,000	
	Accts. Receivable - Bunn Co.		6,000
	Received a $6,000, 30-day, 12% note.		

Date	Description	Debit	Credit
Dec. 21	Cash	6,060	
	Notes Receivable		6,000
	Interest Revenue		60
	Collected amount due on note dated November 21.		

Principal + Interest = Maturity Value
$$\$6,000 + (\$6,000 \times 12\% \times 30 / 360) = \$6,060$$

Practice:

You have received a $160,000, 90-day note, with interest of 11.5%. How much will you collect at the maturity date?

Understanding the 360-Day Year

- ✔ In commercial transactions it is traditional to use a 360-day year.

- ✔ The historic rationale for this procedure was ease of calculation, which made sense before the computer and calculator age.

- ✔ Why does this practice continue when most small calculators and desktop computers can present complex interest calculations in a few seconds?

Why does it?

Another Look at the 360-Day Year

1. Assume a $100,000 note dated June 1 for 90 days at an interest rate of 12 percent. The textbook calculation is as follows:

   $100,000 x (12 / 100) x (90 /360) = $3,000.00

2. A more precise calculation is as follows:

   $100,000 x (12 / 100) x (90 /365) = $2,958.90

3. When large sums are involved the 360-day method (known as ordinary interest or banker's rule) yields significantly more interest to the lender. It is used by banks and commercial organizations.

4. The second method (known as exact interest) is used by the federal government and the Federal Reserve System.

Who benefits by using the 360-day year? The lender or the borrower?

Notes:

Crabtree Co.
Balance Sheet
December 31, 20--

Assets

Current assets:

Cash		$119,500
Notes receivable		250,000
Accounts receivable	$445,000	
Less allowance for		
doubtful accounts	15,000	430,000
Interest receivable		14,500

Is the $15,000 an actual amount that will not be collected?

Solvency Measures — The Short-Term Creditor

Accounts Receivable Turnover

	2000	1999
Net sales on account	$1,498,000	$1,200,000
Accounts receivable (net):		
Beginning of year	$ 120,000	$ 140,000
End of year	115,500	120,000
Total	$ 235,000	$ 260,000
Average	$ 117,500	$ 130,000
Accts. receivable turnover	12.7 times	9.2 times

Use: To assess the efficiency in collecting receivables and in the management of credit

Notes:

Solvency Measures — The Short-Term Creditor

Number of Days' Sales in Receivables

	2000	1999
Net sales on account	$1,498,000	$1,200,000
Accounts receivable (net):		
Beginning of year	$ 120,000	$ 140,000
End of year	115,500	120,000
Total	$ 235,000	$ 260,000
Average	$ 117,500	$ 130,000
Average collection period	28 days	36 days

How are these numbers calculated?

Use: To assess the efficiency in collecting receivables and in the management of credit

Notes:

True / False Questions

True False

____ ____   1. All receivables that are expected to be realized in cash within a year are presented in the current assets section of the balance sheet.

____ ____   2. Notes receivable due in 3 years are presented in the current assets section of the balance sheet.

____ ____   3. Since receivables record keeping and credit approval do not involve cash, there is no need to separate these duties for internal control.

____ ____   4. The interest on a 12%, 60-day note for $10,000 is $1,200.

____ ____   5. The due date of a 60-day note dated July 10 is September 10.

____ ____   6. The maturity value of a 12%, 60-day note for $10,000 is $10,200.

____ ____   7. The party promising to pay a note at maturity is the payee.

____ ____   8. The discounting of a note receivable creates a contingent liability that continues in effect until the due date of the note.

____ ____   9. If the maker of a note fails to pay the debt on the due date, the note is said to be dishonored.

____ ____   10. The difference between Accounts Receivable and its contra asset account is called net realizable value.

____ ____   11. The allowance method and the direct write-off method are both methods of aging accounts receivable.

____ ____   12. Temporary investments in debt securities are carried in the accounts at the lower of cost or market.

Instructions:

Place a check mark in the appropriate column.

Multiple Choice Questions

____ 1. A note receivable due in 90 days is listed on the balance sheet under the caption:
  a. long-term liabilities
  b. plant assets
  c. current assets
  d. current liabilities

____ 2. A note receivable due in 5 years is listed on the balance sheet under the caption:
  a. current assets   b. investments   c. plant assets   d. owner's equity

____ 3. In reference to a promissory note, the person who makes the promise to pay is called the:
  a. maker   b. payee   c. seller   d. payor

____ 4. In reference to a promissory note, the person who is to receive payment is called the:
  a. maker   b. payee   c. seller   d. payor

____ 5. The amount of a promissory note is called the:
  a. realizable value   b. maturity value   c. face value   d. proceeds

____ 6. The due date of a 90-day note dated July 1 is:
  a. September 30   b. September 28   c. September 29   d. October 1

____ 7. If the maker of a promissory note fails to pay the debt on the due date, the note is said to be:
  a. displaced   b. disallowed   c. dishonored   d. discounted

____ 8. A 60-day, 12% note for $15,000, dated May 1, is received from a customer on account. The maturity value of the note is:
  a. $16,200   b. $14,700   c. $15,000   d. $15,300

____ 9. Allowance for Doubtful Accounts has a credit balance of $400 at the end of the year (before adjustment), and uncollectible accounts expense is estimated at 1% of net sales. If net sales are $300,000, the amount of the adjusting entry to record the provision for doubtful accounts is:
  a. $3,400   b. $400   c. $2,600   d. $3,000

Instructions:
Enter the letter of the best answer in the space provided.

Power Notes

Learning Objectives

1. Internal Control of Inventories
2. Effect of Inventory Errors
3. Inventory Cost Flow Assumptions
4. Perpetual Inventory Costing Methods
5. Periodic Inventory Costing Methods
6. Comparing Inventory Costing Methods
7. Inventory Valuation Other Than Cost
8. Balance Sheet Presentation of Merchandise
9. Estimating Inventory Cost
10. Financial Analysis and Interpretation

Power Note Topics

- Inventory Control and Relationships
- Perpetual Inventory Accounting
- LIFO and FIFO Cost Flow Assumptions
- Inventory at Lower-of-Cost-or-Market
- Retail and Gross Profit Methods
- Inventory Turnover Ratio

Notes:

Why is Inventory Control Important?

✔ **Inventory is a significant asset and for many companies the largest asset.**

✔ **Inventory is central to the main activity of merchandising and manufacturing companies.**

✔ **Mistakes in determining inventory cost can cause critical errors in financial statements.**

✔ **Inventory must be protected from external risks (such as fire and theft) and internal fraud by employees.**

Notes:

Inventory Costs and Relationships

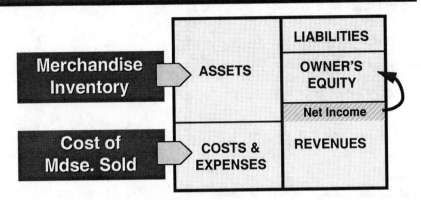

If merchandise inventory is . . . . overstated

Cost of merchandise sold is . . . . . .

Gross profit and net income are . . .

Ending owner's equity is . . . .

If merchandise inventory is . . . . understated

Cost of merchandise sold is . . . . . .

Gross profit and net income are . . .

Ending owner's equity is . . . .

Notes:

Merchandising and Inventory

- ✔ Merchandising involves selling inventory.
- ✔ Inventory is usually an important asset.
- ✔ Inventory must be accounted for <u>periodically</u> or <u>perpetually</u>.
- ✔ Traditional periodic method is often being replaced by <u>perpetual</u> inventory accounting.

Advantages of Using Perpetual Inventory

- ✔ Continuous determination of _Inventory value_
- ✔ Continuous determination of _gross profit_
- ✔ _Affordable_ with computers, scanners, and bar codes on most products
- ✔ Perpetual inventory accounting provides management _controls_
- ✔ Managers know which items are selling fastest and the profit margin on those items.

Notes:

Chapter 9

Perpetual Inventory Costs

Inventory cost data to demonstrate FIFO and LIFO Perpetual Systems

Item 127B		Units	Cost	Price
Jan. 1	Inventory	10	$20	
4	Sale	7		$30
10	Purchase	8	21	
22	Sale	4		30
28	Sale	2		30
30	Purchase	10	22	

Sale price assumptions are added to demonstrate journal entries and ease of calculating gross profit.

Notes:

FIFO Perpetual Inventory Account

Item 127B

Date	Purchases Qty.	Purchases Unit Cost	Purchases Total Cost	Cost of Mdse. Sold Qty.	Cost of Mdse. Sold Unit Cost	Cost of Mdse. Sold Total Cost	Inventory Balance Qty.	Inventory Balance Unit Cost	Inventory Balance Total Cost
Jan 1							10	20	200
4				7	20	140	3	20	60
10	8	21	168				3	20	60
							8	21	168
22				3	20	60			
				1	21	21	7	21	147
28				2	21	42	5	21	105
30	10	22	220				5	21	105
							10	22	220
Totals	18		$388	13		$263	15		$325

Date	Description	Debit	Credit
Jan. 31			
	To record January sales of Item 127B. (7 units@$30, 4 units@$30, 2 units@$30)		
Jan. 31			
	To record cost of January sales of Item 127B.		

— Record the entry.

— Record the entry.

Notes:

LIFO Perpetual Inventory Account

Item 127B

Date	Purchases Qty.	Unit Cost	Total Cost	Cost of Mdse. Sold Qty.	Unit Cost	Total Cost	Inventory Balance Qty.	Unit Cost	Total Cost
Jan 1							10	20	200
4				7	20	140	3	20	60
10	8	21	168				3	20	60
							8	21	168
22				4	21	84	3	20	60
							4	21	84
28				2	21	42	3	20	60
							2	21	42
30	10	22	220				3	20	60
							2	21	42
							10	22	220
Totals	18		$388	13		$266	15		$322

Date	Description	Debit	Credit
Jan. 31			
	To record January sales of Item 127B. (7 units@$30, 4 units@$30, 2 units@$30)		
Jan. 31			
	To record cost of January sales of Item 127B.		

— Record the entry.

— Record the entry.

Notes:

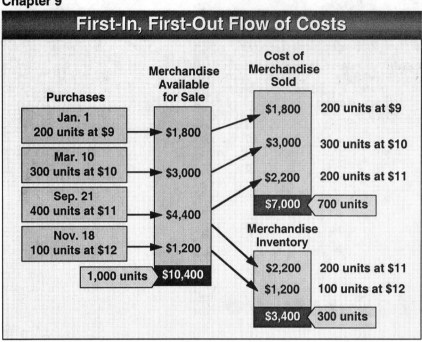

First-In, First-Out Flow of Costs

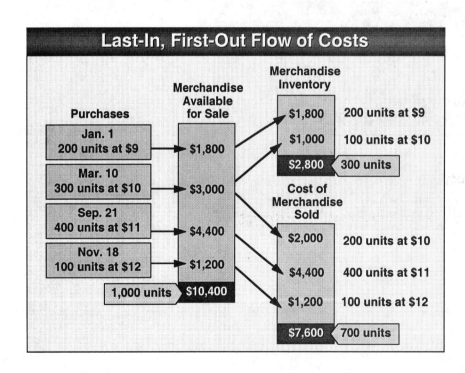

Last-In, First-Out Flow of Costs

Valuation of Inventory at Lower-of-Cost-or-Market

Item	Inventory Quantity	Unit Cost Price	Unit Market Price	Total Cost	Total Market	Lower C or M
A	400	$10.25	$ 9.50	$ 4,100	$ 3,800	
B	120	22.50	24.10	2,700	2,892	
C	600	8.00	7.75	4,800	4,650	
D	280	14.00	14.75	3,920	4,130	

____ Complete these and total the three columns

Afro-Arts
Balance Sheet
December 31, 2001

Assets

Current assets:

Cash		$ 19,400
Accounts receivable	$80,000	
Less allowance	3,000	77,000
Merchandise inventory at lower of cost (first-in, first-out method) or market		216,300

Notes:

Retail Method of Estimating Inventory Cost

- ✔ Retail method is based on relationship between cost of merchandise available for sale and the retail price.
- ✔ Retail prices of all merchandise must be accumulated.
- ✔ Inventory at retail is calculated as retail price of merchandise available for sale less sales.
- ✔ Ratio is calculated as cost divided by retail price.
- ✔ Inventory at retail price times cost ratio equals estimated cost of inventory.

Retail Inventory Method Calculation

	Cost	Retail
Merchandise inventory, January 1	$19,400	$36,000
Purchases in January (net)	42,600	64,000
Merchandise available for sale		
Ratio of cost to retail price:		
Sales for January (net)		70,000
Merchandise inventory, January 31, at retail		_____
Merchandise inventory, January 31, at est. cost		_____

Calculate and enter the missing numbers.

Chapter 9

Gross Profit Method of Estimating Inventory Cost

1. A gross profit percentage rate is estimated based on previous experience, adjusted for known changes.
2. Estimated gross profit is calculated by multiplying the estimated gross profit rate times the actual net sales.
3. Estimated cost of merchandise sold is calculated by subtracting the gross profit from actual sales.
4. The cost of merchandise sold estimate is deducted from actual merchandise available for sale to determine the estimated cost of merchandise inventory.

Gross Profit Method Calculation

Merchandise inventory, January 1		$ 57,000
Purchases in January (net)		180,000
Merchandise available for sale		
Sales in January (net)	$250,000	
Less: Estimated gross profit	————	
Estimated cost of merchandise sold		————
Estimated merchandise inventory, January 31		————

Calculate and enter the missing numbers.

Inventory Turnover Ratios

	SUPERVALU	La-Z-Boy
Cost of goods sold	$15,040,117,000	$ 705,379,000
Inventories:		
Beginning of year	$1,113,937,000	$81,091,000
End of year	1,109,791,000	79,192,000
Total	$2,223,728,000	$ 160,283,000
Average	$1,111,864,000	$80,141,500
Inventory turnover	13.5 times	8.8 times
Average selling period	27 days	41 days

Use: To assess the efficiency in the management of inventory

Is this what the textbook refers to as **Number of days' sales in inventory**?

Notes:

True / False Questions

True False

_____ _____ 1. Merchandise inventory is usually presented on the balance sheet immediately following receivables.

_____ _____ 2. If the cost of units purchased and the prices at which they were sold remained stable, all three inventory methods would yield the same results.

_____ _____ 3. The two principal systems of inventory accounting are periodic and physical.

_____ _____ 4. When the rate of inflation is high, the larger gross profits that result are frequently called inventory profits.

_____ _____ 5. If merchandise inventory at the end of the period is understated, gross profit will be overstated.

_____ _____ 6. As used in the phrase lower-of-cost-or-market, "market" means selling price.

_____ _____ 7. If merchandise inventory at the end of the period is overstated, owner's equity at the end of the period will be understated.

_____ _____ 8. During a period of rising prices, the inventory costing method which will result in the highest amount of net income is lifo.

_____ _____ 9. When the retail inventory method is used, inventory at retail is converted to cost on the basis of the ratio of cost to replacement cost of the merchandise available for sale.

_____ _____ 10. When terms of a sale are FOB destination, title usually does not pass to the buyer until the commodities are delivered.

_____ _____ 11. A company using the perpetual inventory system does not need to take a physical count.

_____ _____ 12. In valuing damaged merchandise for inventory purposes, net realizable value is the estimated selling price plus any direct cost of disposition.

_____ _____ 13. If the retail inventory method is used, inventory figures can be provided for interim statements without the necessity of taking a physical inventory.

_____ _____ 14. Of the three widely used inventory costing methods (fifo, lifo, and average), the average method is the most widely used.

Instructions:

Place a check mark in the appropriate column.

Multiple Choice Questions

____ 1. Merchandise inventory at the end of the year was understated. Which of the following statements correctly states the effect of the error?
   a. Gross profit is understated
   b. Net income is overstated
   c. Cost of merchandise sold is understated
   d. Beginning inventory of the next year is overstated

____ 2. Taking a physical count of inventory:
   a. is not necessary when a periodic inventory system is used
   b. is a detective control
   c. has no internal control relevance
   d. is not necessary when a perpetual inventory system is used

____ 3. Under which method of inventory cost flows is the cost flow assumed to be in the reverse order in which the expenditures were made?
   a. weighted average
   b. last-in, first-out
   c. first-in, first-out
   d. average cost

____ 4. Under which method of cost flows is the inventory assumed to be composed of the most recent costs?
   a. weighted average
   b. last-in, first-out
   c. first-in, first-out
   d. average cost

____ 5. If merchandise inventory is being valued at cost and the price level is steadily rising, the method of costing that will yield the highest net income is:
   a. periodic
   b. lifo
   c. fifo
   d. average cost

____ 6. If the replacement price of an item of inventory is lower than its cost, the use of the lower of cost or market method:
   a. is not permitted unless a perpetual inventory system is maintained
   b. is recommended in order to maximize the reported net income
   c. tends to overstate the gross profit
   d. reduces gross profit for the period in which the decline occurred

Instructions:
Enter the letter of the best answer in the space provided.

Power Notes

Fixed Assets and Intangible Assets

Learning Objectives

1. Nature of Fixed Assets
2. Accounting for Depreciation
3. Capital and Revenue Expenditures
4. Disposal of Fixed Assets
5. Leasing Fixed Assets
6. Internal Control of Fixed Assets
7. Natural Resources
8. Intangible Assets
9. Financial Reporting
10. Financial Analysis and Interpretation

Power Note Topics

- Fixed Assets and Depreciation
- Depreciation Methods
- Capital and Revenue Expenditures
- Disposal of Fixed Assets
- Leasing Fixed Assets
- Depletion and Amortization
- Balance Sheet Presentation
- Fixed Assets to Long-Term Debt

Notes:

Nature of Fixed Assets

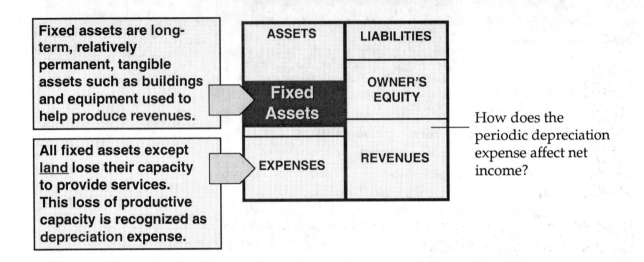

Fixed assets are long-term, relatively permanent, tangible assets such as buildings and equipment used to help produce revenues.

All fixed assets except <u>land</u> lose their capacity to provide services. This loss of productive capacity is recognized as depreciation expense.

How does the periodic depreciation expense affect net income?

Factors that Determine Depreciation Expense

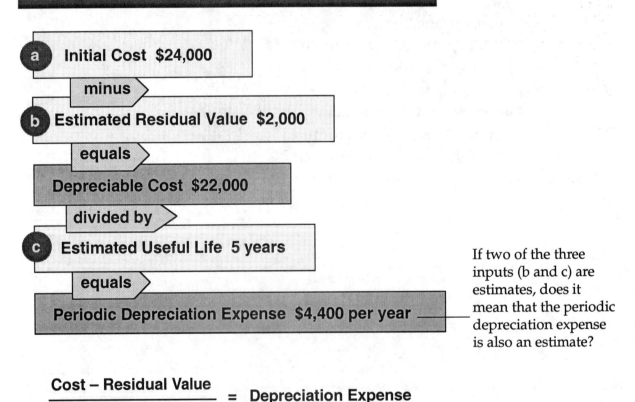

a Initial Cost $24,000

minus

b Estimated Residual Value $2,000

equals

Depreciable Cost $22,000

divided by

c Estimated Useful Life 5 years

equals

Periodic Depreciation Expense $4,400 per year

If two of the three inputs (b and c) are estimates, does it mean that the periodic depreciation expense is also an estimate?

$$\frac{\text{Cost} - \text{Residual Value}}{\text{Estimated Useful Life}} = \text{Depreciation Expense}$$

Costs of Acquiring Plant Assets Include:

- ✔ Sales tax and freight costs
- ✔ Installation and assembling
- ✔ Repairs and reconditioning (used assets)
- ✔ Testing and modifying
- ✔ Insurance while asset is in transit

Why isn't sales tax treated as an expense?

Costs of Acquiring Plant Assets Exclude:

- ✔ Vandalism and uninsured theft
- ✔ Mistakes in installation
- ✔ Damage during unpacking and installing

Notes:

Recording Depreciation

A Purchase equipment for $24,000. Estimated residual value is $2,000 and useful life is 5 years.

B Record straight-line depreciation for first year.

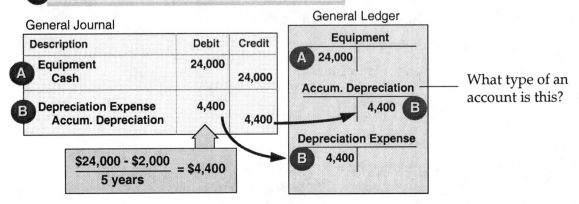

General Journal

Description	Debit	Credit
A Equipment	24,000	
Cash		24,000
B Depreciation Expense	4,400	
Accum. Depreciation		4,400

$$\frac{\$24{,}000 - \$2{,}000}{5 \text{ years}} = \$4{,}400$$

General Ledger

Equipment
A 24,000

Accum. Depreciation
4,400 B

Depreciation Expense
B 4,400

What type of an account is this?

Calculation of Book Value

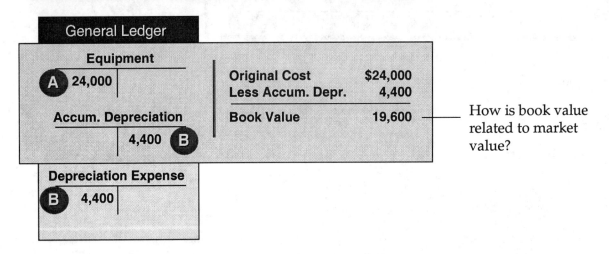

General Ledger

Equipment
A 24,000

Accum. Depreciation
4,400 B

Depreciation Expense
B 4,400

Original Cost	$24,000
Less Accum. Depr.	4,400
Book Value	19,600

How is book value related to market value?

Notes:

Depreciation Methods

The following four depreciation methods are acceptable for <u>Financial Accounting</u> purposes:
1. <u>Straight-Line</u>
2. <u>Units-of-Production</u>
3. <u>Declining-Balance</u>
4. <u>Sum-of-Years-Digits</u>

<u>Straight-line</u> is far more widely used than other methods.

<u>Declining-balance</u> and <u>sum-of-years-digits</u> are known as accelerated depreciation methods.

Comparing Depreciation Methods

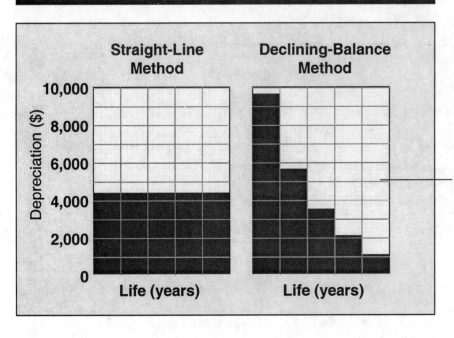

What are the advantages and disadvantages of using the declining-balance method?

Straight - Line Depreciation

Year	Cost	Accum. Depr. at Beginning of Year	Book Value at Beginning of Year	Depr. Expense for Year	Book Value at End of Year
1	$24,000		$24,000.00	$4,400.00	$19,600.00
2	24,000	$ 4,400.00	19,600.00	4,400.00	15,200.00
3	24,000	8,800.00	15,200.00	4,400.00	10,800.00
4	24,000	13,200.00	10,800.00	4,400.00	6,400.00
5	24,000	17,600.00	6,400.00	4,400.00	2,000.00

$$\frac{\text{Cost (\$24,000) - Residual Value (\$2,000)}}{\text{Estimated Useful Life (5 years)}} = \text{Annual Depreciation Expense (\$4,400)}$$

Declining - Balance Depreciation

Year	Cost	Accum. Depr. at Beginning of Year	Book Value at Beginning of Year	Rate	Depr. Expense for Year	Book Value at End of Year
1	$24,000		$24,000.00	40%	$9,600.00	$14,400.00
2	24,000	$ 9,600.00	14,400.00	40%	5,760.00	8,640.00
3	24,000	15,360.00	8,640.00	40%	3,456.00	5,184.00
4	24,000	18,816.00	5,184.00	40%	2,073.60	3,110.40
5	24,000	20,889.60	3,110.40	—	1,110.40	2,000.00

How is the last year's amount calculated?

Note the acceleration of depreciation expense into early years of the life of the asset.

Notes:

Capital and Revenue Expenditures

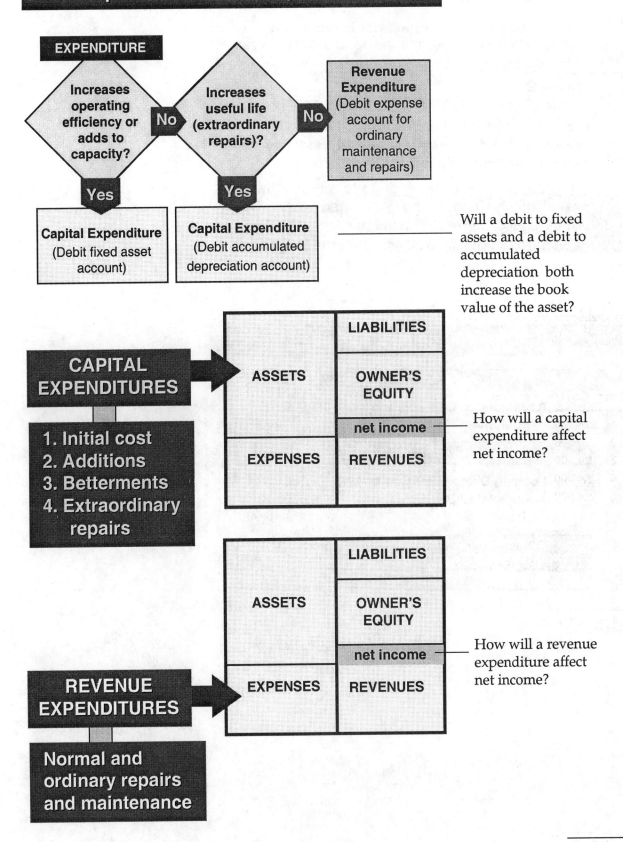

EXPENDITURE

Increases operating efficiency or adds to capacity? — No → Increases useful life (extraordinary repairs)? — No → Revenue Expenditure (Debit expense account for ordinary maintenance and repairs)

Yes ↓

Capital Expenditure (Debit fixed asset account)

Yes ↓

Capital Expenditure (Debit accumulated depreciation account)

Will a debit to fixed assets and a debit to accumulated depreciation both increase the book value of the asset?

CAPITAL EXPENDITURES

1. Initial cost
2. Additions
3. Betterments
4. Extraordinary repairs

ASSETS	LIABILITIES
	OWNER'S EQUITY
	net income
EXPENSES	REVENUES

How will a capital expenditure affect net income?

ASSETS	LIABILITIES
	OWNER'S EQUITY
	net income
EXPENSES	REVENUES

How will a revenue expenditure affect net income?

REVENUE EXPENDITURES

Normal and ordinary repairs and maintenance

Accounting for Fixed Asset Disposals

When fixed assets lose their usefulness they
may be disposed of in one of the following ways:
1. discarded,
2. sold, or
3. traded (exchanged) for similar assets.

Required entries will vary with type of
disposition and circumstances, but the following
entries will always be necessary:

Asset account must be credited to remove the
asset from the ledger, and the related
Accumulated Depreciation account must be
debited to remove its balance from the ledger.

Discarding Fixed Assets

Date	Description	Debit	Credit
Feb. 14	Accumulated Depreciation	25,000	
	Equipment		25,000
	Write off fully depreciated equipment.		
Mar. 24	Loss on Disposal of Equipment	1,100	
	Accumulated Depreciation	4,900	
	Equipment		6,000
	Write off partially depreciated equipment.		

Notes:

Sale of Fixed Assets

When fixed assets are sold, the owner may break even, sustain a loss, or realize a gain.

1. If the sale price is <u>equal to book value</u>, there will be <u>no gain or loss</u>.

2. If the sale price is <u>less than book value</u>, there will be a <u>loss</u> equal to the difference.

3. If the sale price is <u>more than book value</u>, there will be a <u>gain</u> equal to the difference.

Gain or loss will be reported in the income statement as <u>Other Income</u> or <u>Other Loss</u>.

Sale of Fixed Assets

Sold equipment with a book value of $2,250 (cost $10,000, accumulated depreciation $7,750).

Date	Description	Debit	Credit
Oct. 12	Cash	1,000	
	Loss on Disposal of Equipment	1,250	
	Accumulated Depreciation	7,750	
	Equipment		10,000
	Sold below book value, for $1,000.		
Oct. 12	Cash	2,800	
	Accumulated Depreciation	7,750	
	Equipment		10,000
	Gain on Disposal of Equipment		550
	Sold above book value, for $2,800.		

Notes:

Exchanges of Similar Fixed Assets

- ✔ <u>Trade-in Allowance (TIA)</u> – amount allowed for old equipment toward the purchase price of similar new assets.

- ✔ <u>Boot</u> – balance owed on new equipment after trade-in allowance has been deducted.

- ✔ TIA > Book Value = <u>Gain on Trade</u>

- ✔ TIA < Book Value = <u>Loss on Trade</u>

- ✔ **Gains** are <u>never recognized</u> (not recorded).

- ✔ **Losses** <u>must be recognized</u> (recorded).

It seems unfair to not recognize gains. Why is this?

Notes:

Chapter 10

Exchanges of Similar Fixed Assets

Quoted price of new equipment acquired	$15,000
Cost of old equipment traded in	$12,500
Accum. depreciation at date of exchange	10,100
Book value at date of exchange	$ 2,400

Case One (GAIN)
Trade-in allowance, $3,000
Cash paid, $12,000 ($15,000 – $3,000)
TIA > Book Value = Gain
$3,000 – $2,400 = $600
Boot + Book = Cost of New Equipment
$12,000 + $2,400 = $14,400

Gains are not recognized for financial reporting.

Date	Description	Debit	Credit

Record the entry for Case One.

Case Two (LOSS)
Trade-in allowance, $2,000
Cash paid, $13,000 ($15,000 – $2,000)
TIA < Book Value = Loss
$2,000 – $2,400 = $400
Cost of New Equipment =
Quoted Price of New Asset $15,000

Losses are recognized for financial reporting.

Date	Description	Debit	Credit

Record the entry for Case Two.

Natural Resources and Depletion

Depletion is the periodic allocation of the cost of metal ores and other minerals removed from the earth.

Date	Description	Debit	Credit
Dec. 31			

— Record the entry.

Paid $400,000 for the mining rights to a mineral deposit estimated at 1,000,000 tons of ore. During the year, 90,000 tons are mined.

Practice:

We acquired mineral rights for $6,000,000. The deposit is estimated to yield 10,000,000 tons. What is the depletion expense for the first year if 500,000 tons were mined?

Intangible Assets and Amortization

Amortization is the periodic cost expiration of intangible assets which do not have physical attributes and are not held for sale (patents, copyrights, and goodwill, etc).

Date	Description	Debit	Credit
Dec. 31			

— Record the entry.

Paid $100,000 for patent rights. The patent life is 11 years and was issued 6 years prior to purchase date.

Practice:

We acquired a patent for $360,000. The patent was acquired 5 years after the original life of 17 years. What is the annual amortization expense?

Leasing Plant Assets

All leases are either capital leases or operating leases.
Capital leases include one or more of the following:
1. Lease transfers ownership to the lessee at the end of the lease term.
2. An option for a bargain purchase by the lessee.
3. Lease term extends over most of the life of the asset.
4. Lease requires rental payments that approximate fair market value of the asset.

Capital leases are accounted for as if the lessee has purchased the asset. Lessee debits an asset account for the fair market value and credits a long-term liability.
Operating leases are accounted for as rent expense.

Discovery Mining Co.
Balance Sheet
December 31, 20--

Property, plant, and equipment:	Cost	Accum. Depr.	Book Value	
Land	$ 30,000		$ 30,000	
Buildings	110,000	$ 26,000	84,000	
Factory equipment	650,000	192,000	458,000	
Office equipment	120,000	13,000	107,000	
	$910,000	$231,000		$ 679,000
Mineral deposits:	Cost	Accum. Depl.	Book Value	
Alaska deposit	$1,200,000	$ 800,000	$400,000	
Wyoming deposit	750,000	200,000	550,000	
	$1,950,000	$1,000,000		950,000
Total property, plant, and equipment				$1,629,000
Intangible assets:				
Patents				$ 75,000
Goodwill				50,000
Total intangible assets				$125,000

Why don't we have accumulated amortization for intangible assets?

Notes:

Financial Analysis and Interpretation

Ratio of Fixed Assets to Long-Term Liabilities

Procter & Gamble	(in millions)	
	1996	1995
Property, plant, equip. (net)	$11,118	$11,026
Long-term liabilities (debt)	$ 4,670	$5,161
Ratio of fixed assets to long-term liabilities	2.4	2.1

Use: To indicate the margin of safety to long-term creditors

Notes:

True / False Questions

True   False

_____ _____ 1. Fully depreciated assets should be retained in the accounting records until disposal has been authorized and they are removed from service.

_____ _____ 2. In using the declining-balance method, the asset should not be depreciated below the net book value.

_____ _____ 3. The method of depreciation which yields a depreciation charge that varies with the amount of asset usage is known as the units-of-production method.

_____ _____ 4. ACRS depreciation methods permit the use of asset lives that are often much shorter than the actual useful life.

_____ _____ 5. A lease which transfers ownership of the leased asset to the lessee at the end of the lease term should be classified as an operating lease.

_____ _____ 6. Intangible assets are usually reported in the balance sheet in the current assets section.

_____ _____ 7. When an old plant asset is traded in for a new plant asset having a similar use, proper accounting treatment prohibits recognition of a gain.

_____ _____ 8. The cost of repairing damage to a machine during installation is debited to a plant asset account.

_____ _____ 9. The periodic decrease in the market value of plant assets is called depreciation.

_____ _____ 10. The accumulated depreciation account is an expense account.

_____ _____ 11. Expenditures that add to the utility of a plant asset for more than one accounting period are capital expenditures.

_____ _____ 12. Expenditures that increase operating efficiency or capacity for the remaining useful life of an asset are revenue expenditures.

_____ _____ 13. A gain can be realized when a plant asset is discarded.

_____ _____ 14. Minerals removed from the earth are classified as intangible assets.

_____ _____ 15. The declining-balance method is NOT an accelerated depreciation method.

_____ _____ 16. The lessor owns the leased property.

Instructions:

Place a check mark in the appropriate column.

Multiple Choice Questions

____ 1. A characteristic of a plant asset is that it is:
a. intangible
b. used in the operations of a business
c. held for sale in the ordinary course of the business
d. not currently used in the business but held for future use

____ 2. Which of the following is included in the cost of constructing a building?
a. Interest incurred during construction
b. Cost of paving parking lot
c. Cost of repairing vandalism damage during construction
d. Cost of removing a building existing on the land when it was purchased

____ 3. Factors contributing to a decline in the usefulness of a plant asset may be divided into the following two categories:
a. salvage and functional
b. physical and functional
c. residual and salvage
d. functional and residual

____ 4. A plant asset's estimated value at the time it is to be retired from service is called:
a. book value
b. residual value
c. market value
d. carrying value

____ 5. Accumulated Depreciation:
a. is used to show the amount of cost expiration of intangibles
b. is the same as Depreciation Expense
c. is a contra asset
d. is used to show the amount of cost expiration of natural resources

____ 6. The most widely used depreciation method is:
a. sum-of-the-years-digits
b. declining-balance
c. units-of-production
d. straight-line

Instructions:
Enter the letter of the best answer in the space provided.

Chapter 11

Power Notes

Current Liabilities

Learning Objectives

1. The Nature of Current Liabilities
2. Short-Term Notes Payable
3. Contingent Liabilities
4. Payroll and Payroll Taxes
5. Accounting Systems for Payroll
6. Employees' Fringe Benefits
7. Financial Analysis and Interpretation

Power Note Topics

- Short-Term Notes Payable
- Product Warranty Liability
- Payroll and Payroll Taxes
- Employees' Earnings
- Employer's Payroll Taxes
- Payroll System and Data Flow
- Quick Ratio

Notes:

Short-Term Notes Payable

Bowden Co. (Buyer/Borrower)		
Description	Debit	Credit
Mdse. Inventory	10,000	
Accts. Payable		10,000
Accts. Payable	10,000	
Notes Payable		10,000
Notes Payable	10,000	
Interest Expense	200	
Cash		10,200

Coker Co. (Seller/Creditor)		
Description	Debit	Credit
Accts. Receivable	10,000	
Sales		10,000
Cost of Mdse. Sold	7,500	
Mdse. Inventory		7,500
Notes Receivable	10,000	
Accts. Receivable		10,000
Cash	10,200	
Interest Revenue		200
Notes Receivable		10,000

July 30. Bowden Co. paid the amount due.
Interest: $10,000 x 12% x 60 / 360 = $200

Practice:

You are the maker of a $150,000, 90-day note, with interest of 11.5%.
How much will you owe on the maturity date of the note?

Product Warranty Liability

To match revenues and expenses properly, warranty costs should be recognized as expenses in the same period in which related revenues are recorded.

Date	Description	Debit	Credit
Dec. 31			

____ Record the appropriate journal entry.

Sales of $60,000 with a 36-month warranty.
Estimated average cost to repair defects is 5%.

Payroll and Payroll Taxes

Payroll is the amount paid to employees for services provided. Payrolls are important because:

1. Good employee relations demand that payrolls be calculated accurately and paid as scheduled.
2. Payroll expenditures are subject to a variety of federal, state, and local taxes.
3. Total payroll expense (gross payroll plus payroll taxes) has a major impact on net income.

Gross Pay Calculation

John T. McGrath is employed by McDermott Supply Co. at the rate of $25 per hour, plus 1.5 times the normal hourly rate for hours over 40 per week. For the week ended December 27, McGrath worked 44 hours.

Employee viewpoint:

Base earnings (40 x$25)	$1,000
Overtime earnings (4 x $37.50)	150
Total earnings	$1,150

Employer viewpoint:

Base earnings (44 x$25)	$1,100
Overtime premium (4 x $12.50)	50
Total earnings	$1,150

Same total earnings but a different view of the overtime hours

Practice:
Calculate total earnings for 48 hours at $20 per hour.

FICA Tax Calculation

Assume that John T. McGrath's annual earnings prior to the current period total $69,150. The current period earnings are $1,150.

FICA tax calculation:

Earnings subject to 6.0% social security tax

($70,000 - $69,150)	$850	
Social security tax rate	x 6%	
Social security tax		$51.00

Earnings subject to 1.5% Medicare tax

Current earnings	$1,150	
Medicare tax rate	x 1.5%	
Medicare tax		17.25
Total FICA tax		$68.25

Practice:
You have earned $69,200 prior to the current period. The current period earnings are $2,000. Calculate your FICA tax, using the rates and limits shown above.

Chapter 11

Withholding Taxes, Other Deductions

Employers are required to withhold <u>federal income tax</u> from each employee based on the withholding table and information provided by the employee's W-4 form.

Federal income tax and FICA tax must be withheld from the pay of each employee.

Deductions for other purposes may be withheld by mutual agreement.

Employee Net Pay Calculation

Earnings:

Regular earnings	$1,000.00	
Overtime earnings	150.00	
Total		$1,150.00

Deductions:

Social security tax tax	$ 51.00	
Medicare tax	17.25	
Federal income tax	237.00	
Retirement savings	20.00	
United Way	5.00	
Total deductions		330.25
Net pay		$ 819.75

John T. McGrath is single, has declared one withholding allowance, and had gross pay of $1,150 for the week ended December 27.

Payroll Register Summary

Earnings:

Regular	$13,328.00	
Overtime	574.00	
Total		$13,902.00

Deductions:

Social security tax	$ 643.07	
Medicare tax	208.53	
Federal income tax	3,332.00	
Retirement savings	680.00	
United Way	470.00	
Accounts receivable	50.00	
Total		5,383.60
Net amount paid		$ 8,518.40

Accounts debited:

Sales Salaries Expense	$11,122.00
Office Salaries Expense	2,780.00
Total (as above)	$13,902.00

Employer's Payroll Taxes

In addition to the amounts due employees, the employer must calculate and pay the following:

1. FICA tax must be paid by the employer on the earnings of each employee.

2. Employers must pay federal unemployment compensation tax at the rate of .8% (.008) on the first $7,000 of annual earnings of each employee.

3. Employers in most states also pay state unemployment compensation tax based on claims experience at a rate not to exceed 5.4% (.054) of the first $7,000 of annual earnings.

Recording Employees' Earnings

Date	Description	Debit	Credit
12/27	Sales Salaries Expense	11,122.00	
	Office Salaries Expense	2,780.00	
	Social Security Tax Payable		643.07
	Medicare Tax Payable		208.53
	Employees Fed. Inc. Tax Payable		3,332.00
	Retirement Savings Deductions Payable		680.00
	United Way Deductions Payable		470.00
	Accounts Receivable–Fred G. Elrod		50.00
	Salaries Payable		8,518.40

Are these taxes always the same for both the employee and employer?

Recording Employer's Payroll Taxes

General Journal

Date	Description	Debit	Credit
12/27	Payroll Tax Expense	1,019.62	
	Social Security Tax Payable		643.07
	Medicare Tax Payable		208.53
	State Unemployment Tax Payable		146.34
	Federal Unemployment Tax Payable		21.68

Question:
What is the total amount of payroll costs for the employer?

Flow of Data in a Payroll System

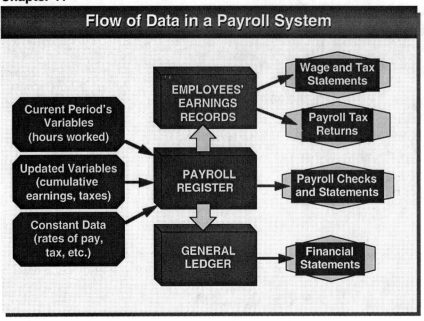

Solvency Measures — Quick Ratio

	Noble Co.	Hart Co.
Quick assets:		
Cash	$ 100,000	$ 55,000
Cash equivalents	47,000	65,000
Accounts receivable (net)	84,000	472,000
Total	$231,000	$592,000
Current liabilities	$220,000	$740,000
Quick ratio	1.05	.8

Use: To indicate instant debt-paying ability

True / False Questions

True   False

____	____	1. Depending on when it is to be paid, vacation liability may be classified in the balance sheet as either a current liability or a long-term liability.
____	____	2. The payroll register may be used as a posting medium.
____	____	3. All states require that unemployment compensation taxes be withheld from employees' pay.
____	____	4. In order for revenues and expenses to be matched properly, a liability to cover the cost of a product warranty must be recorded in the period when the product is repaired.
____	____	5. If pension cost is partially funded, the employer's contribution to a pension plan for normal pension cost for a given year is recorded by a debit to Pension Expense and credits to Cash and Unfunded Pension Liability.
____	____	6. All changes in the constants of the payroll system, such as changes in pay rates, should be properly authorized in writing.
____	____	7. All payroll taxes levied against employers become liabilities at the time the related payroll is paid to employees.
____	____	8. Only employers are required to contribute to the Federal Insurance Contributions Act program.
____	____	9. The total earnings of an employee for a payroll period are called gross pay.
____	____	10. The amounts withheld from employees' earnings have an effect on the firm's debits to the salary or wage expense accounts.
____	____	11. The recording procedures when special payroll checks are used are different from the procedures when the checks are drawn on the regular bank account.
____	____	12. The form used to maintain a cumulative record of each employee's earnings is called the payroll register.
____	____	13. The net amount available to the borrower from discounting a non-interest-bearing note payable is called the discount.

Instructions:

Place a check mark in the appropriate column.

Multiple Choice Questions

_____ 1. For which of the following taxes is there no ceiling on the amount of employee annual earnings subject to the tax?
a. Only federal income tax
b. Only FICA tax
c. Only federal unemployment compensation tax
d. Only state unemployment compensation tax

_____ 2. An employee's rate of pay is $8 per hour, with time and a half for hours worked in excess of 40 during a week. If the employee works 50 hours during a week and has FICA tax withheld at a rate of 7.5% and federal income tax withheld at a rate of 15%, the employee's net pay for the week is:
a. $440
b. $374
c. $341
d. $310

_____ 3. Which of the following items would not be considered a fringe benefit?
a. Vacations
b. Employee pension plans
c. Health insurance
d. FICA benefits

_____ 4. For good internal control over payroll, which of the following is not desirable?
a. all payments are made in cash
b. all additions of employees are authorized in writing
c. attendance records are controlled
d. employee identification cards are used for clocking in

_____ 5. The interest deducted from discounting a non-interest-bearing note payable is called:
a. proceeds
b. discount
c. face value
d. maturity value

_____ 6. Vacation pay payable is reported on the balance sheet as:
a. current liability or long-term liability, depending upon when the vacation will be taken by employees
b. current liability
c. owner's equity
d. long-term liability

Instructions:
Enter the letter of the best answer in the space provided.

Power Notes

Learning Objectives

1. Nature of a Corporation
2. Stockholders' Equity
3. Sources of Paid-in Capital
4. Issuing Stock
5. Treasury Stock Transactions
6. Stock Splits **C12**
7. Accounting for Dividends
8. Financial Analysis and Interpretation

Power Note Topics

- Characteristics of Corporations
- Stockholders' Equity
- Issuing Stock
- Treasury Stock Transactions
- Stock Splits and Dividends
- Dividend Yield on Common Stock

Notes:

Characteristics of Corporations

- ✔ **As a separate legal entity, a corporation may own and dispose of property in its own name.**
- ✔ **The corporation ownership is divided into units called shares of stock.**
- ✔ **The owners of the shares are called shareholders or stockholders.**
- ✔ **Stockholders of a corporation have a limited liability.**

What is the extent of the stockholders' liability?

Stockholders
(owners of corporation stock)

Classes of Stock

Common Stock – the basic ownership of stock with rights to vote in election of directors, share in distribution of earnings, and purchase additional shares.

Preferred Stock – A class of stock with preferential rights over common stock in payment of dividends and company liquidation.

Stockholders
(owners of corporation stock)

Board of Directors
(elected by stockholders)

In addition to hiring the corporate officers, what are the responsibilities of the board of directors?

Officers
(selected by board of directors)

Can officers and employees also be stockholders?

Employees
(hired by officers)

Forming a Corporation

- ◆ First step is to file an <u>application of incorporation</u> with the state.
- ◆ Because state laws differ, corporations often organize in states with more favorable laws.
- ◆ More than half of the largest companies are incorporated in <u>Delaware</u>.
- ◆ State grants a <u>charter</u> or <u>articles of incorporation</u> which formally create the corporation.
- ◆ <u>Management</u> and <u>board of directors</u> prepare <u>bylaws</u> which are operation rules and procedures.

Why is Delaware so popular?

Cost of organizing includes legal fees, taxes and licenses, promotion costs, etc. These costs are recorded as an intangible asset.

Date	Description	Debit	Credit
Jan. 5	Organization Costs	8,500	
	Cash		8,500
	Paid organization costs of $8,500.		
Dec. 31	Amortization Expense	1,700	
	Organization Costs		1,700
	Amortization of organization costs over 5 years.		

$8,500 costs / 5 years = $1,700

If the corporation is assumed to have an undetermined life, why are the organization costs spread over 5 years?

Stockholders' Equity

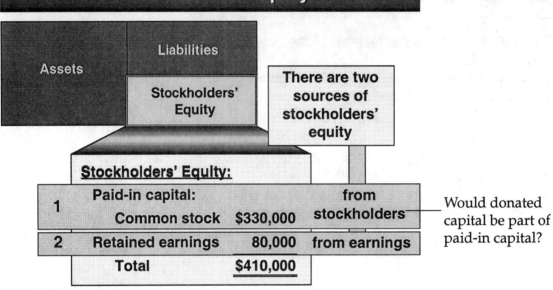

There are two sources of stockholders' equity

Stockholders' Equity:

1	Paid-in capital:		from stockholders
	Common stock	$330,000	
2	Retained earnings	80,000	from earnings
	Total	$410,000	

Would donated capital be part of paid-in capital?

Two Classes of Stockholders

Common Stock –
The basic ownership of stock includes:
1. <u>Right to vote</u> in election of directors and other important matters.
2. <u>Right to share</u> in distribution of <u>earnings</u>.
3. <u>Preemptive right</u> to purchase sufficient shares of new common stock offerings to maintain an existing ownership percentage.

Preferred Stock –
A class of stock with preferential rights over common stock with respect to <u>payment of dividends</u> and assets of the coproration in <u>liquidation</u>.

Why do preferred stockholders *not* have voting rights?

Nonparticipating Preferred Stock

A nonparticipating preferred stock is limited to a certain amount. Assume 1,000 shares of $4 nonparticipating preferred stock and 4,000 shares of common stock and the following:

	1999	2000	2001
Net income	$20,000	$55,000	$62,000
Amount retained	10,000	20,000	40,000
Amount distributed	$10,000	$35,000	$22,000
Preferred dividend	4,000	4,000	4,000
Common dividend	$6,000	$31,000	$18,000
Dividends per share:			
Preferred	$ 4.00	$ 4.00	$ 4.00
Common	$ 1.50	$ 7.75	$ 4.50

Cumulative Preferred Stock

Assume 1,000 shares of $4 <u>cumulative preferred stock</u> and 4,000 shares of common stock. No dividends have been paid in the preceding two years.

Amount distributed in 3rd year		$22,000
Preferred Dividend:		
First year in arrears	$4,000	
Second year in arrears	4,000	
Third year current	4,000	12,000
Common dividend		$10,000
Dividends per share:		
Preferred		$ 12.00
Common		$ 2.50

Who decides if preferred stock is cumulative?

Premium on Issuing Stock

When stock is issued for more than its par, the stock has sold at a <u>premium</u>. It has sold at a <u>discount</u> if issued for less than its par.

Date	Description	Debit	Credit
Jan. 5	Cash	110,000	
	Preferred Stock		100,000
	Paid-In Capital in Excess		10,000

Issued 2,000 shares of $50 par preferred stock for $55.

The $10,000 excess is recorded in a <u>separate account</u> because some states do <u>not</u> consider this to be part of legal capital and may be used for dividends.

Many states do <u>not permit</u> issuance at a discount.

Notes:

Issuing Stock for Non-Cash Assets

Stock issued for assets other than cash should be recorded at the fair market value of the asset or fair market value of the stock, whichever can be more clearly determined.

Date	Description	Debit	Credit
Jan. 5	Land	120,000	
	Common Stock		100,000
	Paid-In Capital in Excess		20,000

Acquired land (fair market value cannot be determined) for 10,000 shares of $10 par common. The current market price of the stock is $12 per share.

Issuing No-Par Stock

In most states, both preferred and common stock may be issued without a par value. Preferred stock, however, is normally assigned a par value.

Date	Description	Debit	Credit
Jan. 5	Cash	400,000	
	Common Stock		400,000

Issuance of 10,000 shares of no-par common at $40.

Date	Description	Debit	Credit
Jun. 15	Cash	36,000	
	Common Stock		36,000

Issuance of 1,000 shares of no-par common at $36.

Treasury Stock Transactions

A recent survey indicated that over 64% of companies reported treasury stock.

Treasury stock is stock that:
1. Has been issued as fully paid.
2. Has been reacquired by the corporation.
3. Has not been canceled or reissued.

A commonly used method of accounting for treasury stock is the cost method.

The account **Treasury Stock** is debited for a purchase.

When sold, Treasury Stock is credited and any difference is debited or credited to an account titled **Paid-In Capital from Sale of Treasury Stock.**

Treasury Stock Transactions

Date	Description	Debit	Credit
Jan. 5	Treasury Stock	45,000	
	Cash		45,000
	Purchased 1,000 shares of treasury stock at $45.		
Jun. 2	Cash	12,000	
	Treasury Stock		9,000
	Paid-In Capital–Treasury Stock		3,000
	Sold 200 shares of treasury stock at $60.		
Sep. 3	Cash	8,000	
	Paid-In Capital–Treasury Stock	1,000	
	Treasury Stock		9,000
	Sold 200 shares of treasury stock at $40.		

Why isn't this revenue?

General Ledger

Account: Treasury Stock					Account No. 380
				Balance	
Date	Item	Debit	Credit	Debit	Credit
1/5	1,000 shs.@ $45	45,000		45,000	
6/2	200 shs. @ $60		9,000	36,000	
9/3	200 shs. @ $40		9,000	27,000	

Is this balance the remaining 600 shares at $45 per share?

Account: Paid-In Capital Treasury Stock					Account No. 395
				Balance	
Date	Item	Debit	Credit	Debit	Credit
6/2	200 shs. @ $60		3,000		3,000
9/3	200 shs. @ $40	1,000			2,000

If treasury stock is sold for more than its cost, the difference is credited to Paid-In Capital Treasury Stock.

Stockholders' Equity		
Paid-in capital:		
Common stock, $25 par		
(20,000 shares authorized and issued)	$500,000	
Excess of issue price over par	150,000	
From sale of treasury stock	2,000	
Total paid-in capital		$652,000
Retained earnings		130,000
Total		$782,000
Deduct treasury stock (600 shares at cost)		27,000
Total stockholders' equity		$755,000

Debit balance of Treasury Stock account.

Accounting for Stock Splits

Corporations sometimes reduce the par or stated value of their common stock by issuing a proportionate number of additional shares. This is called a <u>stock split</u>.

<u>An example:</u>
A corporation has 10,000 shares of $100 par common stock outstanding when a 5-for-1 stock split is declared.

Before:
   100,000 shares @ $100 par = <u>$10,000,000</u>

After:
   500,000 shares @ $20 par = <u>$10,000,000</u>

The <u>total legal capital</u> is the same. Only the number of shares and the par per share are changed. No journal entry is required.

The total legal capital is the same, but what effect will the stock split have on the market price per share?

Notes:

Dividends

- ✔ Dividends are <u>distributions of retained earnings</u> to stockholders.
- ✔ Dividends may be paid in <u>cash</u>, <u>stock</u>, or <u>property</u>.
- ✔ Dividends, even on cumulative preferred stock, are <u>never required</u>, but once declared become a <u>legal liability</u> of the corporation.
- ✔ Cash dividends are declared and paid on shares outstanding, with three conditions:
  1. Sufficient retained earnings
  2. Sufficient cash
  3. Formal action by the board of directors

Accounting for Cash Dividends

A quarterly cash dividend is declared on 5,000 shares of $100 par, 10% preferred stock and $0.30 on the 100,000 shares of $10 par common stock.

Date	Description	Debit	Credit
Dec. 1	Cash Dividends	42,500	
	Cash Dividends Payable		42,500
	Declared cash dividends on preferred and common. Preferred: $2.50 x 5,000 shares = $12,500 Common: $0.30 x 100,000 shares = $30,000		
Jan. 2	Cash Dividends Payable	42,500	
	Cash		42,500
	Paid cash dividend declared on December 1.		

What type of account is Cash Dividends?

Accounting for Stock Dividends

Stock dividends transfer pro rata shares of stock to stockholders. Assume a 5% stock dividend on common stock, $20 par, 2,000,000 shares issued.

Date	Description	Debit	Credit
Dec. 15	Stock Dividends	3,100,000	
	Stock Dividends Distributable		2,000,000
	Paid-In Capital in Excess of Par		1,100,000

Declared a 100,000 (5%) stock dividend on common. Market price is $31 a share at declaration date.

Date	Description	Debit	Credit
Jan. 10	Stock Dividends Distributable	2,000,000	
	Common Stock		2,000,000

Issued the stock dividend declared on December 15.

What type of account is Stock Dividends?

Stock Dividends and Stockholders' Equity

	Before	After
Common stock	$40,000,000	$42,000,000
Excess of issue price over par	9,000,000	10,100,000
Retained earnings	26,600,000	23,500,000
Total stockholders' equity	$75,600,000	$75,600,000
Number of shares outstanding	2,000,000	2,100,000
Equity per share	$37.80	$36.00
A Stockholder:		
Shares owned	1,000	1,050
Total equity	$37,800	$37,800
Portion of corporation owned	.05%	.05%

Note: The individual stockholder's equity is the same before and after the stock dividend, although the total number of shares have increased by 5%.

Profitability Measures — The Common Stockholder

Dividend Yield

	2000	1999
Dividends per share of common	$ 0.80	$ 0.60
Market price per share of common	$20.50	$13.50
Dividend yield on common stock	3.9%	4.4%

Use: To indicate the rate of return to common stockholders in terms of dividends

True / False Questions

True	False		
_____	_____	1.	The financial loss that each stockholder in a corporation can incur is limited to the amount invested by the stockholder.
_____	_____	2.	Cash dividends paid by a corporation from earnings are not taxed as income to stockholders receiving them.
_____	_____	3.	Changes in ownership terminate the life of a corporation.
_____	_____	4.	The stockholders' equity section of the balance sheet is divided into three major subdivisions: common stock, paid-in capital, and retained earnings.
_____	_____	5.	If 20,000 shares are authorized, 15,000 shares are issued, and 500 shares are held as treasury stock, the number of outstanding shares is 14,500.
_____	_____	6.	Preferred stock with a preferential right to assets on liquidation is referred to as participating preferred.
_____	_____	7.	The paid-in capital in excess of par account has a debit balance.
_____	_____	8.	When a corporation issues stock at a premium, it reports the premium as an other income item on the income statement.
_____	_____	9.	The primary purpose of a stock split is to reduce the number of shares outstanding in order to encourage more investors to enter the market for the company's shares.
_____	_____	10.	A corporation has 10,000 shares of $25 par value stock outstanding that has a current market value of $100. If the corporation issues a 5-for-1 stock split, the market value of the stock will fall to approximately $20.
_____	_____	11.	The declaration of a cash dividend decreases a corporation's stockholders' equity and increases its liabilities.
_____	_____	12.	Cash dividends become a liability to a corporation on the date of record.
_____	_____	13.	The declaration and issuance of a stock dividend does not affect the total amount of a corporation's assets, liabilities, or stockholders' equity.
_____	_____	14.	When a stock dividend is declared, it becomes a liability.

Instructions:

Place a check mark in the appropriate column.

Multiple Choice Questions

____ 1. Which of the following is characteristic of a corporation?
   a. The stockholders have unlimited liability
   b. When stockholders sell their shares, the corporation is dissolved
   c. A corporation cannot own property in its name
   d. Cash dividends paid by a corporation are taxable to the shareholders

____ 2. Organization Costs is included on the balance sheet as a (n):
   a. plant asset   b. intangible asset   c. investment   d. current asset

____ 3. A debit balance in retained earnings is called:
   a. paid-in capital   b. paid-in capital in excess of par
   c. deficit   d. contra asset

____ 4. Preferred stock that provides for the payment of preferred dividends that have
   been passed (are in arrears) before dividends may be paid on common stock is
   called:
   a. par   b. cumulative   c. no-par   d. participating

____ 5. The charter of a corporation provides for the issuance of 100,000 shares of
   common stock. Assume that 40,000 shares were originally issued and 5,000 were
   subsequently reacquired. What is the number of shares outstanding?
   a. 35,000   b. 45,000   c. 55,000   d. 5,000

____ 6. A corporation purchases 1,000 shares of its $10 par common stock at $20 and
   subsequently sold 500 of the shares at $30. What is the amount of revenue
   realized from the sale?
   a. $2,500   b. $5,000   c. $15,000   d. $0

____ 7. The primary purpose of a stock split is to:
   a. increase paid-in capital   b. reduce the market price of the stock per share
   c. increase the market price of the stock per share   d. increase retained earnings

____ 8. The entry to record the declaration of a common stock dividend would include a
   credit to:
   a. Common Stock   b. Retained Earnings
   c. Stock Dividends Distributable   d. Cash

Instructions:
Enter the letter of the best answer in the space provided.

Chapter 13

Power Notes

Corporations: Income and Taxes, Stockholders' Equity, Investments in Stocks

Learning Objectives
 C13

1. Corporate Income Taxes
2. Unusual Income Statement Items
3. Earnings Per Common Share
4. Reporting Stockholders' Equity
5. Comprehensive Income
6. Accounting for Investment in Stocks
7. Business Combinations
8. Financial Analysis and Interpretation

Power Note Topics

- Corporate Income Taxes
- Unusual Income Statement Items
- Earnings Per Common Share
- Reporting Stockholders' Equity
- Long-Term Stock Investments
- Business Combinations
- Price-Earnings Ratio

Notes:

Corporate Income Taxes

- ✔ Corporations are <u>taxable entities</u> that must pay income taxes.

- ✔ Because income tax is often a significant amount, it is reported as a special deduction.

- ✔ <u>Taxable income</u> is determined according to tax laws which are often different from <u>income before income tax</u> according to GAAP.

- ✔ Differences in tax law and GAAP create some <u>temporary differences</u> that reverse in later years.

- ✔ Temporary differences do not change or reduce the total amount of tax paid; they affect only the timing of when the taxes are paid.

If taxable income is different from financial accounting income, are two sets of books necessary?

Temporary Differences in Reporting Revenues

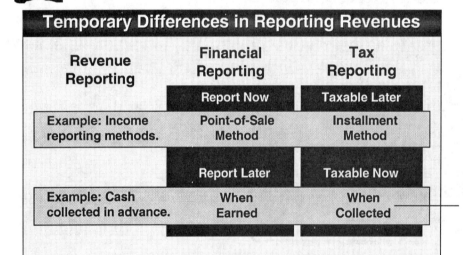

Revenue Reporting	Financial Reporting	Tax Reporting
	Report Now	**Taxable Later**
Example: Income reporting methods.	Point-of-Sale Method	Installment Method
	Report Later	**Taxable Now**
Example: Cash collected in advance.	When Earned	When Collected

Does the IRS tax this even if it hasn't been earned?

Temporary Differences in Reporting Expenses

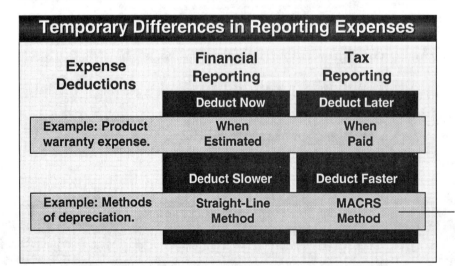

Expense Deductions	Financial Reporting	Tax Reporting
	Deduct Now	**Deduct Later**
Example: Product warranty expense.	When Estimated	When Paid
	Deduct Slower	**Deduct Faster**
Example: Methods of depreciation.	Straight-Line Method	MACRS Method

Why does the IRS allow a faster deduction?

Income Tax Accounting

Financial reporting and tax reporting summary:
Income before tax $300,000 x 40% rate = $120,000
Taxable income $100,000 x 40% rate = $40,000

Date	Description	Debit	Credit
1st Yr.	Income Tax Expense	120,000	
	Income Tax Payable		40,000
	Deferred Income Tax Payable		80,000

Income tax allocation due to timing differences.

Date	Description	Debit	Credit
2nd Yr.	Deferred Income Tax Payable	48,000	
	Income Tax Payable		48,000

Record $48,000 of deferred tax as payable.

How is deferred income tax reported on the financial statements?

Notes:

Unusual Income Statement Items

Three types of <u>unusual items</u> are:

1. **Results of discontinued operations.**
2. **Extraordinary items of gain or loss.**
3. **A change from one generally accepted accounting principle to another.**

These items and the <u>related tax effects</u> are reported separately in the income statement.

Why are these items reported separately?

Jones Corporation
Income Statement
For the Year Ended December 31, 2000

Net sales	$9,600,000
Income from continuing operations before income tax	$1,310,000
Income tax	620,000
Income from continuing operations	$ 690,000
Loss on discontinued operations (Note A)	100,000
Income before extraordinary items and cumulative effect of a change	
Extraordinary item: Gain on condemna applicable income tax of $65,000	150,000
Cumulative effect on prior years of changing to different depreciation method (Note B)	92,000
Net income	$832,000

Differences created by unusual items: discontinued operations, extraordinary items, and change in methods.

Notes:

Reporting Earnings Per Common Share

Earnings per share (EPS) is the net income per share of common stock outstanding. When unusual items exist, EPS should be reported for:

1. Income from <u>continuing operations</u>.
2. Income before extraordinary items and the cumulative effect of a change in accounting principle.
3. Extraordinary items and the cumulative effect of a change in accounting principle.
4. <u>Net income</u>.

Jones Corporation
Income Statement
For the Year Ended December 31, 2000

Income from continuing operations	$690,000
Net income	$832,000
Earnings per common share:	
Income from continuing operations	$ 3.45
Loss on discontinued operations	.50
Income before extraordinary item and cumulative effect of a change in accounting principle	2.95
Extraordinary item	.75
Cumulative effect on prior years of changing to a different depreciation method	.46
Net income	$ 4.16

Notes:

Stockholders' Equity		
Paid-in capital:		
Preferred $5 stock, cumulative, $50 par		
(2,000 shares authorized and issued)	$100,000	
Excess of issue price over par	10,000	$ 110,000
Common stock, $20 par		
(50,000 shares authorized, 45,000 issued)	$900,000	
Excess of issue price over par	132,000	1,032,000
From donated land		60,000
Total paid-in capital		$1,202,000

Shareholders' Equity		
Contributed capital:		
Preferred 10% stock, cumulative, $50 par		
(2,000 shares authorized and issued)	$100,000	
Common stock, $20 par		
(50,000 shares authorized, 45,000 issued)	$900,000	
Additional paid-in capital	202,000	
Total contributed capital		$1,202,000

Reporting Retained Earnings

Adang Corporation
Retained Earnings Statement
For the Year Ended June 30, 2000

Retained earnings, July 1, 1999		$350,000
Net income	$280,000	
Less dividends declared	75,000	
Increase in retained earnings		205,000
Retained earnings, June 30, 2000		$555,000

Notes:

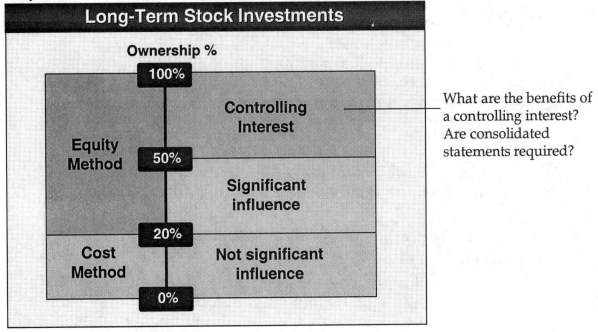

Long-Term Stock Investments

Ownership %

100%

Controlling Interest

Equity Method

50%

Significant influence

20%

Cost Method

Not significant influence

0%

What are the benefits of a controlling interest? Are consolidated statements required?

Notes:

Cost Method

The cost method is used when the buyer does not have significant influence over the operating and financing activities of the investee.

Date	Description	Debit	Credit
Mar. 1	Investment in Stock	5,940	
	Cash		5,940
	Purchased 100 shares of Compton Corp. stock at 59 plus brokerage fee of $40.		
Dec. 31	Cash	200	
	Dividend Revenue		200
	Received $2 cash dividend from Compton Corp.		

Sale of Long-Term Stock Investment

When shares of stock are sold, the investment account is credited for the carrying value (book value) of the shares sold.

Date	Description	Debit	Credit
Mar. 1	Cash	17,500	
	Investment in Stock		15,700
	Gain on Sale of Investments		1,800
	Sold stock of Drey Inc. for $17,500. Stock has a carrying value of $15,700.		

Equity Method

Date	Description	Debit	Credit
Jan. 2	Investment in Brock Corp. Stock	350,000	
	Cash		350,000
	Purchased 40% of Brock Corporation for $350,000.		
Dec. 31	Investment in Brock Corp. Stock	42,000	
	Income of Brock Corp.		42,000
	Brock Corporation reports net income of $105,000.		
Dec. 31	Cash	18,000	
	Investment in Brock Corp. Stock		18,000
	Brock Corporation reports total dividends of $45,000.		

Business Combinations

✔ **Many businesses combine in order to produce more efficiently or to diversify product lines.**

✔ **A <u>merger</u> combines two corporations by one acquiring the properties of another that is then dissolved.**

✔ **A <u>consolidation</u> is the creation of a new corporation, to which the combined assets and liabilities of the old corporations are transferred.**

Is it necessary to have 100% ownership to merge or consolidate?

Mergers

Consolidations

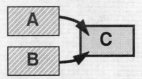

<u>Mergers:</u> **Company A acquires company B. The assets and liabilities of B are transferred to A and B is then dissolved.**

<u>Consolidations:</u> **Company A acquires company B. The assets and liabilities of <u>both</u> A and B are transferred to a new company C, and A and B are then dissolved.**

Analyzing Stock Investments

Accounting: Earnings Per Share

$$\frac{\text{Net Income}}{\text{Common Shares}} = \text{Earnings Per Share}$$

Investing: Price - Earnings Ratio

$$\frac{\text{Market Price Per Share}}{\text{Earnings Per Share}} = \text{Price-Earnings Ratio}$$

Price – Earnings Ratio

The price-earnings ratio represents how much the market is willing to pay per dollar of a company's earnings. This indicates the market's assessment of a firm's growth potential and future earnings prospects.

An example:	1997	1996
Market price per share	$20.50	$13.50
Earnings per share	$1.64	$1.35
Price-earnings ratio	12.5	10.0

The price-earnings ratio indicates that a share of common stock was selling for 10 times earnings for 1996 and 12.5 times for 1997.

Does this mean that the buyer of the stock is willing to pay for ten years of future earnings?

Notes:

True / False Questions

True   False

_____ _____ 1. Deferred income tax is reported in the stockholders' equity section of the balance sheet.

_____ _____ 2. When a corporation discontinues a segment of its operations at a loss, the loss should be reported as a separate item after income from continuing operations on the income statement.

_____ _____ 3. Extraordinary items are events and transactions that are unusual and infrequent in their occurrence.

_____ _____ 4. A difference between estimated and actual warranty expense is considered an error and would be reported as a prior period adjustment.

_____ _____ 5. The price-earnings ratio is commonly quoted in the financial press.

_____ _____ 6. Ordinarily, a corporation owning a significant portion of the voting stock of another corporation accounts for the investment using the equity method.

_____ _____ 7. The investor carrying an investment by the cost method records its share of the periodic net income of the investee as an increase in the investment account.

_____ _____ 8. If a corporation acquired the voting common stock of another corporation in exchange for cash, the transaction is treated as a pooling of interests.

_____ _____ 9. The financial statements resulting from combining parent and subsidiary statements are called consolidated statements.

_____ _____ 10. The minority interest may be reported immediately preceding the stockholders' equity on the consolidated balance sheet.

Instructions:

Place a check mark in the appropriate column.

Multiple Choice Questions

_____ 1. Deferred income tax may be reported on the balance sheet in the:
a. plant assets section   b. intangible assets section
c. current liabilities section   d. current assets section

_____ 2. The income before income tax for the first year of operations is $750,000. Because of timing differences in accounting and tax methods, the taxable income for the same year is $650,000. Assuming an income tax rate of 50%, the amount of the deferred income tax would be:
a. $50,000   b. $100,000   c. $325,000   d. $375,000

_____ 3. A loss on disposal of a segment would be reported in the income statement as a(n):
a. administrative expense   b. other expense
c. deduction from income from continuing operations   d. selling expense

_____ 4. For 1997, net income is $125,000, shares outstanding are 50,000, and the market price is $20. What is the price-earnings ratio on common stock?
a. 8.0   b. 1.25   c. 25   d. 2.5

_____ 5. The receipt of cash dividends on a long-term investment in common stock is accounted for as a debit to Cash and a credit to Dividend Income. Which of the following methods is being used to account for the investment?
a. Market method   b. Cost method
c. Revenue method   d. Equity method

_____ 6. During the year in which Parent Company owned 90% of the outstanding common stock of Subsidiary Company, the subsidiary reported net income of $400,000 and dividends declared and paid of $50,000. What is the amount of net increase in minority interest for the year?
a. $40,000   b. $315,000   c. $360,000   d. $35,000

Instructions:
Enter the letter of the best answer in the space provided.

Power Notes

Bonds Payable and Investments in Bonds

Learning Objectives

1. Financing Corporations
2. Characteristics of Bonds Payable
3. The Present-Value Concept and Bonds Payable
4. Accounting for Bonds Payable
5. Bond Sinking Funds
6. Bond Redemption
7. Investments in Bonds
8. Corporation Balance Sheet
9. Financial Analysis and Interpretation

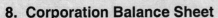

Power Note Topics

- Long-Term Financing
- Characteristics of Bonds Payable
- Time Value of Money
- Issuing Bonds Payable
- Redemption of Bonds Payable
- Investments in Bonds
- Number of Times Interest Earned

Notes:

Two Methods of Long-Term Financing

Resources = Sources

Liabilities

Debt Financing – Bondholders

Assets

Stockholders' Equity

Equity Financing – Stockholders

Why issue bonds rather than stock?

Bonds (debt) – Interest payments to bondholders are an expense that reduces taxable income.

Stock (equity) – Dividend payments are made from aftertax net income and retained earnings.

Earnings per share on common stock can often be increased by issuing bonds rather than additional stock.

Notes:

Alternative Financing Plans – $800,000 Earnings

	Plan 1	Plan 2	Plan 3
12 % bonds	—	—	$2,000,000
Preferred 9% stock, $50 par	—	$2,000,000	1,000,000
Common stock, $10 par	$4,000,000	2,000,000	1,000,000
Total	$4,000,000	$4,000,000	$4,000,000
Earnings before interest and income tax	$ 800,000	$ 800,000	$ 800,000
Deduct interest on bonds	—	—	240,000
Income before income tax	$ 800,000	$ 800,000	$ 560,000
Deduct income tax	320,000	320,000	224,000
Net income	$ 480,000	$ 480,000	$ 336,000
Dividends on preferred stock	—	180,000	90,000
Available for dividends	$ 480,000	$ 300,000	$ 246,000
Shares of common stock	÷ 400,000	÷ 200,000	÷ 100,000
Earnings per share	$ 1.20	$ 1.50	$ 2.46

Alternative Financing Plans – $440,000 Earnings

	Plan 1	Plan 2	Plan 3
12 % bonds	—	—	$2,000,000
Preferred 9% stock, $50 par	—	$2,000,000	1,000,000
Common stock, $10 par	$4,000,000	2,000,000	1,000,000
Total	$4,000,000	$4,000,000	$4,000,000
Earnings before interest and income tax	$ 440,000	$ 440,000	$ 440,000
Deduct interest on bonds	—	—	240,000
Income before income tax	$ 440,000	$ 440,000	$ 200,000
Deduct income tax	176,000	176,000	80,000
Net income	$ 264,000	$ 264,000	$ 120,000
Dividends on preferred stock	—	180,000	90,000
Available for dividends	$ 264,000	$ 84,000	$ 30,000
Shares of common stock	÷ 400,000	÷ 200,000	÷ 100,000
Earnings per share	$ 0.66	$ 0.42	$ 0.30

Notes:

Characteristics of Bonds Payable

✔ <u>Long-term debt</u> – repayable 10, 20, or 30 years after date of issuance.

✔ Issued in face (principal) amounts of $1,000, or multiples of $1,000.

✔ Contract interest rate is <u>fixed</u> for term (life) of the bond.

✔ Face amount of bond repayable at maturity date.

Bond Variables and Constants

1. <u>Constants</u> – fixed by bond contract.
   a. Principal (face) amount.
   b. Contract rate of interest.
   c. Term (life) of the bond.
2. <u>Variables</u> – determined in the bond market.
   a. Market price of the bond.
   b. Market (effective) interest rate.

Notes:

How are Bond Prices Determined

The selling prices of bonds are based on two amounts.

1. Present Value of Face Amount

The present value of the <u>face amount</u> (constant) of the bond at its maturity date, based on the <u>current market interest rate</u> (variable).

2. Present Value of Interest Payments

The present value of the periodic <u>interest payments</u> (constant) for the term of the bonds, based on the <u>current market interest rate</u> (variable).

Market and Contract Interest Rates

Differences in market and bond contract interest rates result in <u>Discounts</u> and <u>Premiums.</u>

When	Bonds sell at
Market rate = Contract rate ➡	Face value
Market rate > Contract rate ➡	Discount
Market rate < Contract rate ➡	Premium

Notes:

The Time Value of Money – Future Value

The time value of money concept is used in many business decisions. This concept is an important consideration in accounting for bonds payable.

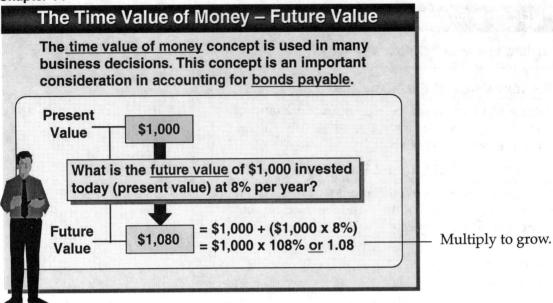

Present Value — $1,000

What is the future value of $1,000 invested today (present value) at 8% per year?

Future Value — $1,080 = $1,000 + ($1,000 x 8%)
= $1,000 x 108% or 1.08

Multiply to grow.

The Time Value of Money – Present Value

The time value of money concept is used in many business decisions. This concept is an important consideration in accounting for bonds payable.

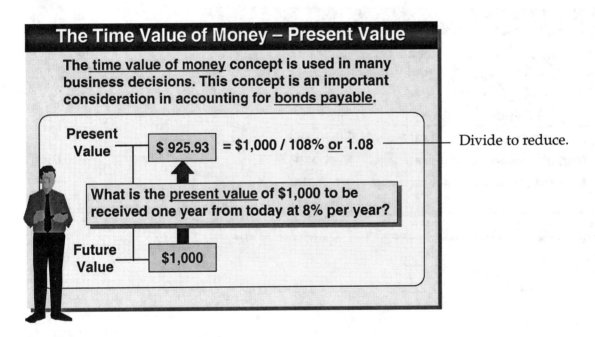

Present Value — $ 925.93 = $1,000 / 108% or 1.08

Divide to reduce.

What is the present value of $1,000 to be received one year from today at 8% per year?

Future Value — $1,000

Notes:

Calculating Present Values

Present values can be determined using present value tables, mathematical formulas, calculators or computers.

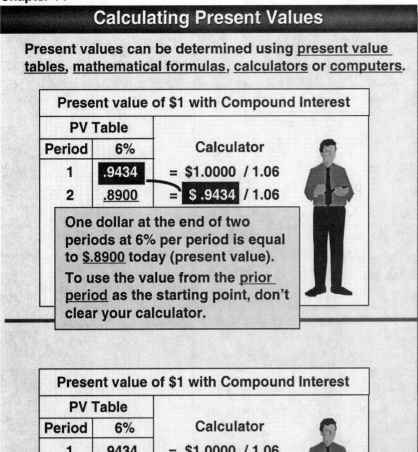

Present value of $1 with Compound Interest

PV Table		Calculator
Period	6%	
1	.9434	= $1.0000 / 1.06
2	.8900	= $ .9434 / 1.06

One dollar at the end of two periods at 6% per period is equal to $.8900 today (present value).

To use the value from the prior period as the starting point, don't clear your calculator.

Present value of $1 with Compound Interest

PV Table		Calculator
Period	6%	
1	.9434	= $1.0000 / 1.06
2	.8900	= $ .9434 / 1.06
3	.8396	= $ .8900 / 1.06
4	.7921	= $ .8396 / 1.06

When using a calculator, learn to use constant division. You will then enter $1 and 1.06 the first time, pressing only the equal (=) key for each successive answer.

Practice:

What is the present value of $80,000 to be received three years from today with interest compounded annually at 9%?

Calculating Present Values of Annuities

Annuities represent a <u>series of equal amounts </u> to be paid or received in the future over equal periods.

Present value of $1 — Annuity of $1			
PV Table		Annuity	Calculation
Period	6%	6%	Sum of Periods
1	.9434	.9434	= Period 1
2	.8900	1.8334	= Periods 1–2
3	.8396	2.6730	= Periods 1–3

The PV of an annuity of $1 to be received each year for three years is $2.6730. This is the sum of the PV of the three amounts for periods 1–3.

Present value of $1 — Annuity of $1			
PV Table		Annuity	Calculation
Period	6%	6%	Sum of Periods
1	.9434	.9434	= Period 1
2	.8900	1.8334	= Periods 1–2
3	.8396	2.6730	= Periods 1–3
4	.7921	3.4651	= Periods 1–4
5	.7473	4.2124	= Periods 1–5
Total	4.2124		

Practice:

What is the present value of $6,000 to be received each year at the end of the next three years with interest compounded annually at 8%?

Cash Flow of Bonds Payable

On January 1, $100,000 of 12%, five-year bonds, with interest of $6,000 payable semiannually are issued. Market rate is 13% at date of issue.

Cash Outflows:		Present Values
Interest payments (10 periods at $6,000)	$ 60,000 =	$ 43,133
Face amount (at end of 5 years)	100,000 =	53,273
	$160,000 =	$96,406
Cash Inflows:		
Selling price	$96,406	

Bonds Issued at Face Amount

On January 1, $100,000 of 12%, five-year bonds, with interest of $6,000 payable semiannually are issued. Market rate is 12% at date of issue.

Date	Description	Debit	Credit
Jan. 1	Cash	100,000	
	Bonds Payable		100,000
	Issued 12%, five-year bonds at face.		

PV of face due in 5 years ($100,000 x 0.55840) = $55,840
PV of $1 for 10 periods at 6%

PV of 10 interest payments ($6,000 x 7.36009) = 44,160
PV of annuity of $1 for 10 periods at 6%
                Total selling price   = $100,000

Notes:

Bonds Issued at a Discount

On January 1, $100,000 of 12%, five-year bonds, with interest of $6,000 payable semiannually are issued. Market rate is 13% at date of issue.

Date	Description	Debit	Credit
Jan. 1	Cash	96,406	
	Discount on Bonds Payable	3,594	
	Bonds Payable		100,000

Issued 12%, five-year bonds at a discount.

PV of face due in 5 years ($100,000 x 0.53273) = $53,273
(PV of $1 for 10 periods at 6.5%)

PV of 10 interest payments ($6,000 x 7.18883) = $43,133
(PV of annuity of $1 for 10 periods at 6.5%)
Total selling price = $96,406

What type of account is Discount on Bonds Payable?

Amortization of a Bond Discount

The straight-line method amortizes bond discount in equal periodic amounts.

Date	Description	Debit	Credit
Jan. 1	Cash	96,406	
	Discount on Bonds Payable	3,594	
	Bonds Payable		100,000

Issued 12%, five-year bonds at a discount.

Date	Description	Debit	Credit
Jun. 30	Interest Expense	6,359.70	
	Discount on Bonds Payable		359.70
	Cash		6,000.00

Payment of semiannual interest and amortization of 1/10 of bond discount.

Bonds Issued at a Premium

On January 1, $100,000 of 12%, five-year bonds, with interest of $6,000 payable semiannually are issued. Market rate is 11% at date of issue.

Date	Description	Debit	Credit
Jan. 1	Cash	103,769	
	Bonds Payable		100,000
	Premium on Bonds Payable		3,769
	Issued 12%, five-year bonds at a premium.		

PV of face due in 5 years ($100,000 x 0.58543) = $ 58,543
(PV of $1 for 10 periods at 5.5%)

PV of 10 interest payments ($6,000 x 7.53763) = 45,226
(PV of annuity of $1 for 10 periods at 5.5%)
            Total PV (selling price)   = $103,769

What type of account is Premium on Bonds Payable?

Amortization of a Bond Premium

The straight-line method amortizes bond premium in equal periodic amounts.

Date	Description	Debit	Credit
Jan. 1	Cash	103,769	
	Bonds Payable		100,000
	Premium on Bonds Payable		3,769
	Issued 12%, five-year bonds at a premium.		
Jun. 30	Interest Expense	5,623.10	
	Premium on Bonds Payable	376.90	
	Cash		6,000.00
	Payment of semiannual interest and amortization of 1/10 of bond premium.		

Zero-Coupon Bonds

Zero-coupon bonds do <u>not provide for interest</u> payments. Only the face amount is paid at maturity. Assume market rate is <u>13%</u> at date of issue.

Date	Description	Debit	Credit
Jan. 1	Cash	53,273	
	Discount on Bonds Payable	46,727	
	Bonds Payable		100,000
	Issued $100,000 five-year zero-coupon bonds.		

PV of face due in 5 years ($100,000 x 0.53273) = $53,273 (PV of $1 for 10 periods at <u>6.5%</u>)

An investment of $53,273 today would yield $100,000 in five years compounded semiannually at 6.5%.

Why would a buyer be interested in bonds that do not pay interest?

Bond Redemption

A corporation may call or redeem its bonds before they mature. Assume a bond issue of $100,000 and an unamortized premium of $4,000. <u>Carrying value</u> is $96,000 and one-fourth of the bonds are purchased.

Date	Description	Debit	Credit
Jun. 30	Bonds Payable	25,000	
	Premium on Bonds Payable	1,000	
	Gain on Redemption of Bonds		2,000
	Cash		24,000
	Redeemed one-fourth of the total bonds.		

Is this reported on the income statement?

Notes:

Investments in Bonds

Bonds are purchased directly from the issuing corporation or through an organized bond exchange. Bond prices are quoted as a percentage of the <u>face amount</u>.

Date	Description	Debit	Credit
Apr. 2	Investment in Bonds	1,025.30	
	Interest Revenue	10.20	
	Cash		1,035.50

Why is Interest Revenue debited?

> Purchased a $1,000 bond at 102 plus a brokerage fee of $5.30 and accrued interest of $10.20

Investors <u>do not usually</u> record premium (or discount) in separate accounts because bonds are not often held until maturity.

Solvency Measures — The Long-Term Creditor

Number of Times Interest Charges Earned

	2000	1999
Income before income tax	$ 900,000	$ 800,000
Add interest expense	300,000	250,000
Amount available for interest	$1,200,000	$1,050,000
Number of times earned	4.0 times	4.2 times

Use: To assess the risk to debtholders in terms of number of times interest charges were earned.

Notes:

True / False Questions

_____ _____   1. Bondholder claims for interest and repayment rank behind the claims of stockholders.

_____ _____   2. When the total amount of a bond issue matures at a certain date, the bonds are called term bonds.

_____ _____   3. The concept of present value is that an amount of cash to be received at some date in the future is not the equivalent of the same amount of cash held at an earlier date.

_____ _____   4. If the market rate of interest is 8% and a corporation's bonds bear interest at 7%, the bonds will sell at a discount.

_____ _____   5. If the market rate of interest is 9% and a corporation's bonds bear interest at 7%, the bonds will sell at a premium.

_____ _____   6. Discount on bonds payable may be amortized by the straight-line method if the results obtained by its use do not materially differ from the results obtained by use of the interest method.

_____ _____   7. If the straight-line method of amortization is used, the amount of unamortized discount on bonds payable will decrease as the bonds approach maturity.

_____ _____   8. The amount of interest expense reported on the income statement will be more than the interest paid to bondholders if the bonds were originally sold at a discount.

_____ _____   9. The amount of interest expense reported on the income statement will be more than the interest paid to bondholders if the bonds were originally sold at a premium.

_____ _____   10. The special fund that is set aside to provide for the payment of bonds at maturity is called a serial fund.

_____ _____   11. There is a gain on redemption of bonds when bonds are redeemed below carrying value.

_____ _____   12. If bonds of $500,000 with unamortized discount of $13,000 are redeemed at 98, the loss on redemption of bonds is $3,000.

_____ _____   13. If the proceeds from the sale of bonds held as a long-term investment exceed the carrying amount of the bonds, a loss is realized.

_____ _____   14. The balance in a bond discount account should be reported in the balance sheet as a deduction from the related bonds payable.

Instructions:

Place a check mark in the appropriate column.

____ 1. Bonds issued on the general credit of the issuing corporation are called:
a. callable bonds   b. serial bonds   c. term bonds   d. debenture bonds

____ 2. The present value of $20,000 to be received in one year, at 5% compounded annually, is (rounded to nearest dollar):
a. $10,000   b. $19,048   c. $20,000   d. $1,000

____ 3. When the contract rate of interest on bonds is higher than the market rate of interest, the bonds sell at:
a. a premium   b. their face value   c. their maturity value   d. a discount

____ 4. The interest rate specified in the bond indenture is called the:
a. discount rate   b. contract rate   c. market rate   d. effective rate

____ 5. The entry to record the amortization of a premium on bonds payable is:
a. debit Premium on Bonds Payable and Interest Expense, credit Cash
b. debit Interest Expense, credit Premium on Bonds Payable
c. debit Interest Expense, credit Cash
d. debit Bonds Payable, credit Interest Expense

____ 6. Sinking Fund Investments would be classified on the balance sheet as:
a. a current asset   b. a plant asset   c. an investment   d. a deferred debit

____ 7. If bonds payable are not callable, the issuing corporation:
a. cannot repurchase them before maturity
b. can repurchase them in the open market
c. must get special permission from the SEC to repurchase them
d. is more likely to repurchase them if the interest rates increase

____ 8. A long-term investment in debt securities is carried at:
a. cost   b. lower of cost or market   c. equity   d. market

____ 9. Bonds with a face value of $50,000 were purchased through a broker at 105 plus accrued interest of $900 and brokerage commission of $60. The amount to be debited to the investment account is:
a. $60   b. $50,000   c. $50,060   d. $52,560

____ 10. On June 1, $500,000 of bonds were purchased as a long-term investment at 99 and $500 was paid as the brokerage commission. If the bonds bear interest at 12%, which is paid semiannually on January 1 and July 1, what is the total cost to be debited to the investment account?
a. $495,500   b. $500,000   c. $500,500   d. $495,000

Instructions:
Enter the letter of the best answer in the space provided.

Learning Objectives

1. Purpose of the Statement of Cash Flows
2. Reporting Cash Flows
3. Statement of Cash Flows – The Indirect Method
4. Statement of Cash Flows – The Direct Method
5. Financial Analysis and Interpretation

C15

Power Note Topics

- Cash Flow Basics
- Statement of Cash Flows – Two Methods
- Changes in Current Accounts
- Statement of Cash Flows – Indirect Method
- Statement of Cash Flows – Direct Method
- Free Cash Flow

Notes:

Reporting Cash Flows

The <u>statement of cash flows</u> reports a firm's major cash inflows and outflows for a period. Cash flows are reported by three types of activities.

1. <u>Operating activities</u> – transactions that affect net income.
2. <u>Investing activities</u> – transactions that affect noncurrent assets.
3. <u>Financing activities</u> – transactions that affect equity and debt of the entity.

Cash Flows – Operating Activities

Typical cash inflows	Typical cash outflows
Sales of goods and services	Merchandise purchases
Interest Revenue	Payments of wages & other expenses
Dividend Revenue	Tax payments

Why is interest revenue, dividend revenue, and interest expense part of operating activities and not financing and investing activities?

Cash Flows – Investing Activities

Typical cash inflows	Typical cash outflows
Sales of fixed assets and other long-term investments	Purchase of fixed assets and other long-term investments
Sale of marketable securities and investments	Purchase of marketable securities and investments

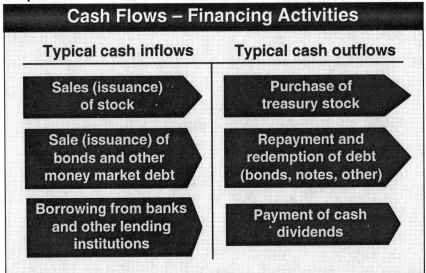

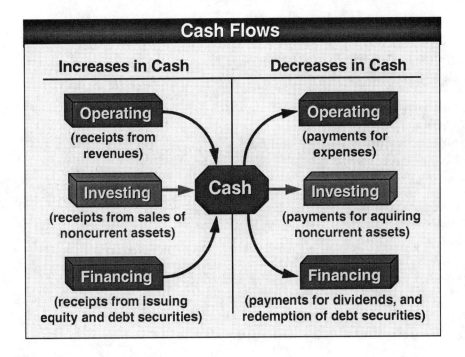

Notes:

Statement of Cash Flows

The statement of cash flows is invaluable in assessing the capacity of a firm to achieve goals such as:

1. Generate cash flow from operations.
2. Maintain and expand operating capacity.
3. Pay dividends.
4. Pay debts, including interest, when due.
5. Generate future profits.

The primary attention is the flow of cash rather than net income.

Preparing the Statement of Cash Flows

Direct Method

Net cash flows from operating activities will be the difference between the operating cash receipts and operating cash payments.

Indirect Method

Net cash flows from operating activities is determined by adjusting the accrual net income from operations to reflect a cash-based net income from operations.

If the direct method is recommended, why do most companies use the indirect method?

Notes:

Advantages of Using the Direct Method

1. Reports the <u>sources</u> and <u>uses</u> of operating cash receipts and payments.

2. Is easier to understand for many investors.

3. Recommended by the Financial Accounting Standards Board (FASB).

   <u>Note:</u> The total amount of net cash flow from operating activities will be the same for both the direct and indirect methods.

   <u>Investing</u> and <u>Financing</u> activities sections will be identical for both methods.

Advantages of Using the Indirect Method

1. Focuses on the differences between <u>net income</u> and <u>net cash flow</u> from operations.

2. Reveals the relationship between the income statement, the balance sheet, and the statement of cash flows.

3. Less costly to prepare.

4. Must be prepared as a supplemental report even if the direct method is used.

5. 98 percent of companies surveyed use the <u>indirect method</u>.

Notes:

Computer King
Statement of Cash Flows – Direct Method
For the Month Ended November 30, 1999

Cash flows from operating activities:

Cash received from customers	$ 7,500
Deduct cash payments for expenses and payment to creditors	4,600
Net cash flow from operating activities	$ 2,900

Is this easier to understand than the indirect method?

Computer King
Statement of Cash Flows – Indirect Method
For the Month Ended November 30, 1999

Cash flows from operating activities:

Net income, per income statement	$ 3,050
Add increase in accounts payable	400
Deduct increase in supplies	(550)
Net cash flow from operating activities	$ 2,900

Cash Relationships and Cash Flows

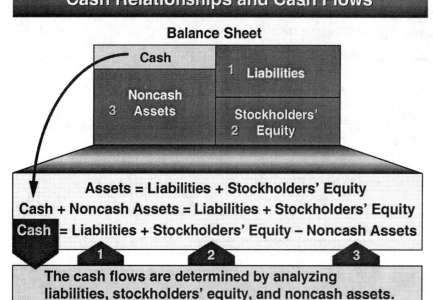

Balance Sheet

Cash

Noncash 3 Assets

1 Liabilities

2 Stockholders' Equity

Assets = Liabilities + Stockholders' Equity

Cash + Noncash Assets = Liabilities + Stockholders' Equity

Cash = Liabilities + Stockholders' Equity – Noncash Assets

The cash flows are determined by analyzing liabilities, stockholders' equity, and noncash assets.

Changes in Current Accounts

Accounts	2000	1999	Change Debit	Change Credit
Trade receivables (net)	$74,000	$65,000	9,000	
Inventories	172,000	180,000		8,000
Accounts payable (mdse.)	43,500	46,700	3,200	
Accrued expenses payable	26,500	24,300		2,200
Income taxes payable	7,900	8,400	500	

These debit changes are subtracted from net income in the operating activities section of the statement of cash flows.

Think of these debits as deductions from net income in arriving at net cash flow from operations.

Changes in Current Accounts

Accounts	2000	1999	Change Debit	Change Credit
Trade receivables (net)	$74,000	$65,000	9,000	
Inventories	172,000	180,000		8,000
Accounts payable (mdse.)	43,500	46,700	3,200	
Accrued expenses payable	26,500	24,300		2,200
Income taxes payable	7,900	8,400	500	

These credit changes are added to net income in the operating activities section of the statement of cash flows.

Think of these credits as additions to net income in arriving at net cash flow from operations.

Notes:

Operating Activities – Indirect Method

Cash flows from operating activities:

Net income, per income statement		$108,000
Add: Depreciation	$ 7,000	
Decrease in inventories	8,000	
Increase in accrued expenses	2,200	17,200
		$125,200
Deduct: Increase in accounts receivables	$ 9,000	
Decrease in accounts payable	3,200	
Decrease in income taxes payable	500	
Gain on sale of land	12,000	24,700
Net cash flow from operating activities		$100,500

Start with the accrual basis net income shown on the income statement.

Operating Activities – Indirect Method

Cash flows from operating activities:

Net income, per income statement		$108,000
Add: Depreciation	$ 7,000	
Decrease in inventories	8,000	
Increase in accrued expenses	2,200	17,200
		$125,200
Deduct: Increase in accounts receivables	$ 9,000	
Decrease in accounts payable	3,200	
Decrease in income taxes payable	500	
Gain on sale of land	12,000	24,700
Net cash flow from operating activities		$100,500

Because depreciation expense reduced net income but did not require an outflow of cash, it is added back to net income.

Notes:

Chapter 15

Operating Activities – Indirect Method

Cash flows from operating activities:

Net income, per income statement		$108,000
Add: Depreciation	$ 7,000	
Decrease in inventories	8,000	
Increase in accrued expenses	2,200	17,200
		$125,200
Deduct: Increase in accounts receivables	$ 9,000	
Decrease in accounts payable	3,200	
Decrease in income taxes payable	500	
Gain on sale of land	12,000	24,700
Net cash flow from operating activities		$100,500

These represent <u>credit changes</u> in the current accounts. Think of these credits as additional income from a cash perspective. Why do these represent an increased cash flow?

Operating Activities – Indirect Method

Cash flows from operating activities:

Net income, per income statement		$108,000
Add: Depreciation	$ 7,000	
Decrease in inventories	8,000	
Increase in accrued expenses	2,200	17,200
		$125,200
Deduct: Increase in accounts receivables	$ 9,000	
Decrease in accounts payable	3,200	
Decrease in income taxes payable	500	
Gain on sale of land	12,000	24,700
Net cash flow from operating activities		$100,500

These represent <u>debit changes</u> in the current accounts. Think of these debits as additional expense from a cash perspective. Why do these represent a reduced cash flow?

Notes:

Operating Activities – Indirect Method

Cash flows from operating activities:

Net income, per income statement			$108,000
Add: Depreciation		$ 7,000	
Decrease in inventories		8,000	
Increase in accrued expenses		2,200	17,200
			$125,200
Deduct: Increase in accounts receivables		$ 9,000	
Decrease in accounts payable		3,200	
Decrease in income taxes payable		500	
Gain on sale of land		12,000	24,700
Net cash flow from operating activities			$100,500

This gain was included in net income but did not represent an operating cash flow. The related cash inflow from the sale is reported in the cash flows from investing activities section.

Operating Activities – Direct Method

Rundell Inc.
Income Statement
For the Year Ended December 31, 2000

Cash Basis

Sales		$1,180,000
Cost of merchandise sold		790,000
Gross profit		$ 390,000
Operating expenses:		
Depreciation expense	$ 7,000	
Other operating expenses	196,000	
Total operating expenses		203,000
Income from operations		$ 187,000
Other income:		
Gain on sale of land	$12,000	
Other expense:		
Interest expense	8,000	4,000
Income before income tax		$ 191,000

This is an accrual basis income statement. The direct method of reporting cash flows will essentially convert this to a cash basis statement.

Notes:

Operating Activities – Direct Method

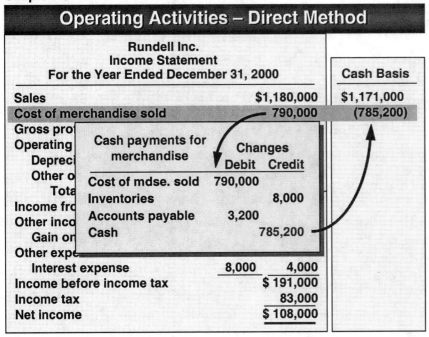

Rundell Inc.
Income Statement
For the Year Ended December 31, 2000

		Cash Basis
Sales	$1,180,000	$1,171,000
Cost of merchandise sold	790,000	(785,200)
Gross pro...		
Operating...		
Depreci...		
Other o...		
Tota...		
Income fr...		
Other inco...		
Gain on...		
Other exp...		
Interest expense	8,000 4,000	
Income before income tax	$ 191,000	
Income tax	83,000	
Net income	$ 108,000	

Cash payments for merchandise

	Changes Debit Credit
Cost of mdse. sold	790,000
Inventories	8,000
Accounts payable	3,200
Cash	785,200

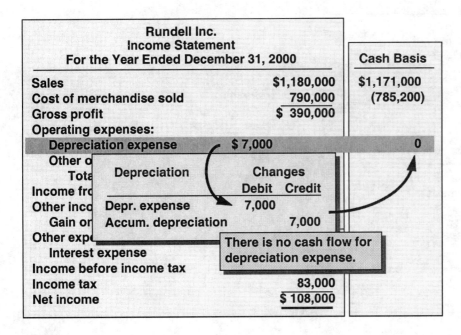

Rundell Inc.
Income Statement
For the Year Ended December 31, 2000

		Cash Basis
Sales	$1,180,000	$1,171,000
Cost of merchandise sold	790,000	(785,200)
Gross profit	$ 390,000	
Operating expenses:		
Depreciation expense	$ 7,000	0
Other o...		
Tota...		
Income fr...		
Other inco...		
Gain on...		
Other exp...		
Interest expense		
Income before income tax		
Income tax	83,000	
Net income	$ 108,000	

Depreciation

	Changes Debit Credit
Depr. expense	7,000
Accum. depreciation	7,000

There is no cash flow for depreciation expense.

Notes:

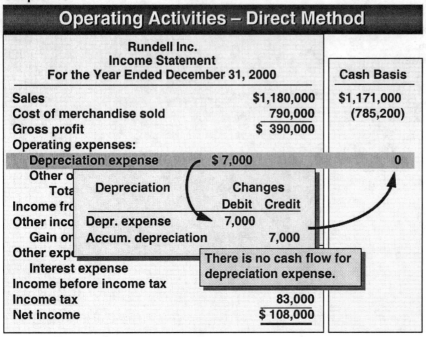

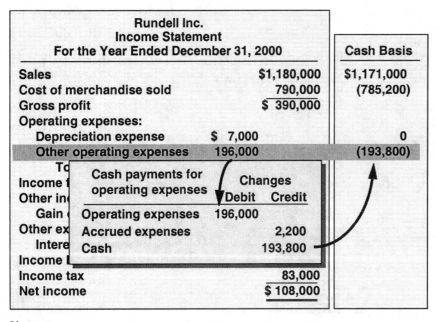

Notes:

Operating Activities – Direct Method

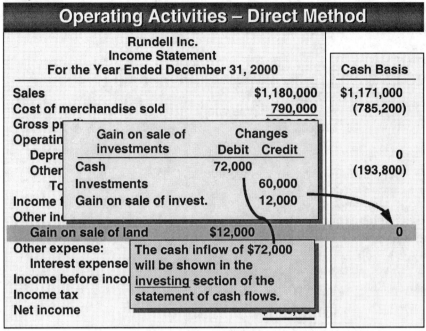

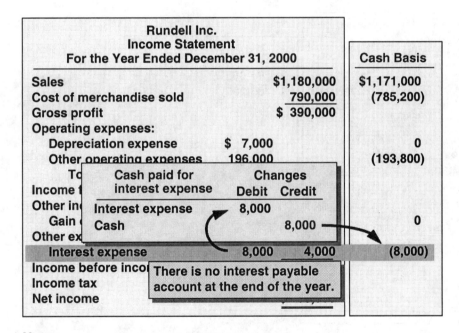

Notes:

Operating Activities – Direct Method

Rundell Inc.
Income Statement
For the Year Ended December 31, 2000

			Cash Basis
Sales		$1,180,000	$1,171,000
Cost of merchandise sold		790,000	(785,200)
Gross profit		$ 390,000	
Operating expenses:			
Depreciation expense	$ 7,000		0
Other operating expenses	196,000		(193,800)
Total operating expenses		203,000	

Cash paid for income taxes		Changes	
		Debit	Credit
Income tax expense		83,000	
Income tax payable		500	
Cash			83,500

		(8,000)	
Income tax		83,000	(83,500)
Net income		$ 108,000	

Rundell Inc.
Income Statement
For the Year Ended December 31, 2000

			Cash Basis
Sales		$1,180,000	$1,171,000
Cost of merchandise sold		790,000	(785,200)
Gross profit		$ 390,000	
Operating expenses:			
Depreciation expense	$ 7,000		0
Other operating expenses	196,000		(193,800)
Total operating expenses		203,000	
Income from operations		$ 187,000	
Other income:			
Gain on sale of land	$12,000		0
Other expense:			
Interest expense	8,000	4,000	(8,000)
Income before income tax		$ 191,000	
Income tax		83,000	(83,500)
Net income		$ 108,000	$ 100,500

Notes:

Operating Activities – Direct Method

Cash flows from operating activities:

Cash inflows:

Cash received from customers		$1,171,000
Cash outflows:		
Cash payments for merchandise	$785,200	
Cash payments for operating expenses	193,800	
Cash payments for interest	8,000	
Cash payments for income tax	83,500	1,070,500
Net cash flow from operating activities		$ 100,500

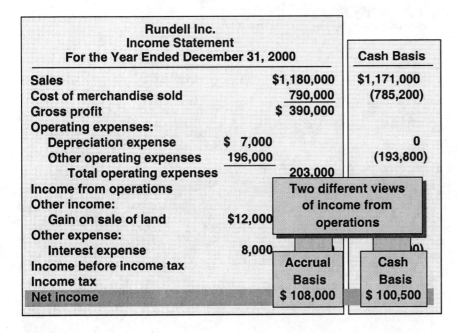

Rundell Inc. Income Statement For the Year Ended December 31, 2000			Cash Basis
Sales		$1,180,000	$1,171,000
Cost of merchandise sold		790,000	(785,200)
Gross profit		$ 390,000	
Operating expenses:			
Depreciation expense	$ 7,000		0
Other operating expenses	196,000		(193,800)
Total operating expenses		203,000	
Income from operations			
Other income:			
Gain on sale of land	$12,000		
Other expense:			
Interest expense	8,000		
Income before income tax			
Income tax			
Net income			

Two different views of income from operations

	Accrual Basis	Cash Basis
Net income	$ 108,000	$ 100,500

Notes:

Financial Analysis and Interpretation

Free Cash Flow

Cash flow from operations	$1,400,000
Less: Cash invested in fixed	
assets to maintain capacity	(450,000)
Less: Cash used for dividends	(100,000)
Free cash flow	$ 850,000

Use: To measure operating cash flow available for corporate purposes after providing sufficient fixed asset additions to maintain current productive capacity and dividends.

Notes:

True / False Questions

_____ _____ 1. The statement of cash flows is an optional financial statement.

_____ _____ 2. Cash flows from investing activities, as part of the statement of cash flows, includes cash transactions that enter into the determination of net income.

_____ _____ 3. Cash flows from financing activities, as part of the statement of cash flows, includes receipts from the issuance of equity securities.

_____ _____ 4. There are two alternatives to reporting cash flows from operating activities in the statement of cash flows: (1) the direct method and (2) the reciprocal method.

_____ _____ 5. The direct method must be used to report cash flows from operating activities in the statement of cash flows.

_____ _____ 6. The main disadvantage of the direct method of reporting cash flows from operating activities is that the necessary data are often costly to accumulate.

_____ _____ 7. If a business issued bonds payable in exchange for land, the transaction would be reported in a separate schedule on the statement of cash flows.

_____ _____ 8. A cash flow per share amount should be reported on the statement of cash flows.

_____ _____ 9. If land costing $100,000 was sold for $150,000, the amount reported in the investing activities section of the statement of cash flows would be $100,000.

_____ _____ 10. If cash dividends of $50,000 were declared during the year and the decrease in dividends payable from the beginning to the end of the year was $2,500, the statement of cash flows would report $52,500 in the financing activities section.

_____ _____ 11. The indirect method reports cash received from customers in the cash flows from operating activities section of the statement of cash flows.

_____ _____ 12. When the indirect method of reporting cash flows from operating activities is used, depreciation is added to net income.

_____ _____ 13. To determine cash received from customers for the cash flow statement using the direct method, decrease in trade receivables is added to sales.

_____ _____ 14. To determine cash payments for merchandise for the cash flow statement using the direct method, decrease in accounts payable is added to cost of merchandise sold.

Instructions:

Place a check mark in the appropriate column.

Multiple Choice Questions

_____ 1. The statement of cash flows reports:
  a. cash flows from operating activities   b. total assets
  c. total changes in stockholders' equity   d. changes in retained earnings

_____ 2. Cash flows from operating activities, as reported on the statement of cash flows, would include:
  a. receipts from the sale of investments   b. payments for dividends
  c. net income   d. receipts from the issuance of capital stock

_____ 3. The last item on the statement of cash flows prior to the schedule of noncash investing and financing activities reports:
  a. the increase or decrease in cash   b. cash at the end of the year
  c. net cash flow from investing activities   d. net cash flow from financing activities

_____ 4. Accounts receivable arising from trade transactions amounted to $35,000 and $40,000 at the beginning and end of the year respectively. Income reported on the income statement for the year was $120,000. Exclusive of the effect of other adjustments, the cash flows from operating activities to be reported on the statement of cash flows prepared by the indirect method is:
  a. $120,000   b. $125,000   c. $155,000   d. $115,000

_____ 5. If a gain of $25,000 is incurred in selling (for cash) office equipment having a book value of $100,000, the total amount reported in the cash flows from investing activities section of the statement of cash flows is:
  a. $75,000   b. $100,000   c. $125,000   d. $25,000

_____ 6. Cash dividends of $80,000 were declared during the year. Cash dividends payable were $25,000 and $20,000 at the beginning and end of the year respectively. The amount of cash for the payment of dividends during the year is:
  a. $75,000   b. $80,000   c. $85,000   d. $60,000

_____ 7. Sales for the year were $500,000. Accounts receivable were $40,000 and $50,000 at the beginning and end of the year. Cash received from customers to be reported on the cash flow statement using the direct method is:
  a. $450,000   b. $460,000   c. $490,000   d. $510,000

_____ 8. Income tax was $200,000 for the year. Income tax payable was $20,000 and $30,000 at the beginning and end of the year. Cash payments for income tax reported on the cash flow statement using the direct method is:
  a. $190,000   b. $200,000   c. $220,000   d. $230,000

Instructions:
Enter the letter of the best answer in the space provided.

Learning Objectives

1. Basic Analytical Procedures
2. Solvency Analysis
3. Profitability Analysis
4. Summary of Analytical Measures
5. Corporate Annual Reports

C16

Power Note Topics

- Horizontal and Vertical Analysis
- Solvency Analysis
- Profitability Analysis
- Annual Reports

Notes:

Lincoln Company
Comparative Balance Sheet
December 31, 2000 and 1999

Assets	2000	1999	Increase (Decrease) Amount	Percent
Current assets	$ 550,000	$ 533,000	$ 17,000	3.2%
Long-term investments	95,000	177,500	(82,500)	(46.5%)
Fixed assets (net)	444,500	470,000	(25,500)	(5.4%)
Intangible assets	50,000	50,000	—	
	$1,139,500	$1,230,500	$ (91,000)	(7.4%)
Liabilities				
Current liabilities	$ 210,000	$ 243,000	$ (33,000)	(13.6%)
Long-term liabilities	100,000	200,000	(100,000)	(50.0%)
	$ 310,000	$ 443,000	$(133,000)	(30.0%)
Stockholders' Equity				
Preferred stock, $100 par	$ 150,000	$ 150,000	—	
Common stock, $10 par	500,000	500,000	—	
Retained earnings	179,500	137,500	$42,000	30.5%
	$ 829,500	$ 787,500	$42,000	5.3%
	$1,139,500	$1230,500	$(91,000)	(7.4%)

Lincoln Company
Comparative Balance Sheet
December 31, 2000 and 1999

Assets	2000	1999	Increase (Decrease) Amount	Percent
Current assets	$ 550,000	$ 533,000	$ 17,000	3.2%
Long-term investments				
Fixed assets (net)				
Intangible assets				
Liabilities				
Current liabilities				
Long-term liabilities				
Stockholders' Equity				
Preferred stock, $100 par	$ 150,000	$ 150,000	—	
Common stock, $10 par	500,000	500,000	—	
Retained earnings	179,500	137,500	$42,000	30.5%
	$ 829,500	$ 787,500	$42,000	5.3%
	$1,139,500	$1230,500	$(91,000)	(7.4%)

Horizontal Analysis:

$$\frac{\text{Current year (2000)} \quad \$550,000}{\text{Base year (1999)} \quad \$533,000} = 103.2\%$$

$$\frac{\text{Increase amount} \quad \$17,000}{\text{Base year (1999)} \quad \$533,000} = 3.2\%$$

Can this be calculated either way?

Notes:

Lincoln Company
Comparative Income Statement
December 31, 2000 and 1999

	2000	1999	Increase (Decrease) Amount	Percent
Sales	$1,530,500	$1,234,000	$296,500	24.0%
Sales returns	32,500	34,000	(1,500)	(4.4%)
Net sales	$1,498,000	$1,200,000	$298,000)	24.8%
Cost of goods sold				
Gross profit				
Selling expenses				
Administrative expenses				
Total operating expenses				
Operating income				
Other income				
Other expense	6,000	12,000	(6,000)	(50.0%)
Income before income tax	$ 162,500	$ 134,600	$ 27,900	20.7%
Income tax	71,500	58,100	13,400	23.1%
Net income	$ 91,000	$ 76,500	$ 14,500	19.0%

Horizontal Analysis:

$$\frac{\text{Current year (2000)} \quad \$1,498,000}{\text{Base year (1999)} \quad \$1,200,000} = 124.8\%$$

$$\frac{\text{Increase amount} \quad \$298,000}{\text{Base year (1999)} \quad \$1,200,000} = 24.8\%$$

Lincoln Company
Comparative Balance Sheets

	December 31, 2000 Amount	Percent	December 31, 1999 Amount	Percent
Assets				
Current assets	$ 550,000	48.3%	$ 533,000	43.3%
Long-term investments	95,000	8.3	177,500	14.4
Fixed assets (net)	444,500	39.0	470,000	38.2
Intangible assets	50,000	4.4	50,000	4.1
	$1,139,500	100.0%	$1,230,500	100.0%
Liabilities				
Current liabilities	$ 210,000	18.4%	$ 243,000	19.7%
			200,000	16.3
			$ 443,000	36.0%
			$ 150,000	12.2%
			500,000	40.6
			137,500	11.2
	$829,500	72.8%	$787,500	64.0%
	$1,139,500	100.0%	$1230,500	100.0%

Vertical Analysis:

$$\frac{\text{Current liabilities} \quad \$210,000}{\text{Total assets} \quad \$1,139,500} = 18.4\%$$

Notes:

Lincoln Company
Comparative Balance Sheets

	December 31, 2000		December 31, 1999	
	Amount	Common-Size Statements		
Assets				
Current assets	$ 550,000	48.3%	$ 533,000	43.3%
Long-term investments	95,000	8.3	177,500	14.4
Fixed assets (net)	444,500	39.0	470,000	38.2
Intangible assets	50,000	4.4	50,000	4.1
	$1,139,500	100.0%	$1,230,500	100.0%
Liabilities				
Current liabilities	$ 210,000	18.4%	$ 243,000	19.7%
Long-term liabilities	100,000	8.8	200,000	16.3
	$310,000	27.2%	$ 443,000	36.0%
Stockholders' Equity				
Preferred stock, $100 par	$ 150,000	13.2%	$ 150,000	12.2%
Common stock, $10 par	500,000	43.9	500,000	40.6
Retained earnings	179,500	15.7	137,500	11.2
	$829,500	72.8%	$787,500	64.0%
	$1,139,500	100.0%	$1230,500	100.0%

Does the "common-size" refer only to the percentages?

Solvency Analysis

Solvency is the ability of a business to meet its financial obligations (debts) as they are due.

Solvency analysis focuses on the ability of a business to pay or otherwise satisfy its current and noncurrent liabilities.

This ability is normally assessed by examining balance sheet relationships.

Notes:

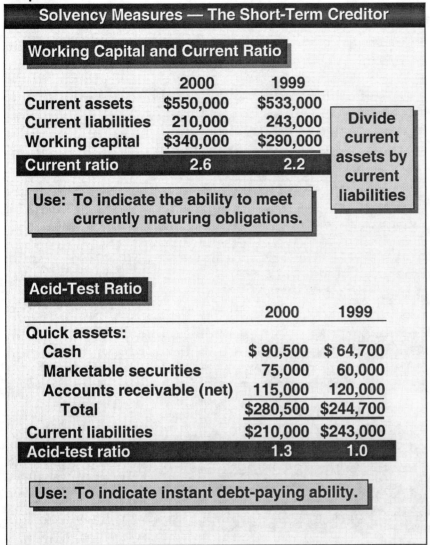

Solvency Measures — The Short-Term Creditor

Working Capital and Current Ratio

	2000	1999
Current assets	$550,000	$533,000
Current liabilities	210,000	243,000
Working capital	$340,000	$290,000
Current ratio	2.6	2.2

Divide current assets by current liabilities

Use: To indicate the ability to meet currently maturing obligations.

Acid-Test Ratio

	2000	1999
Quick assets:		
Cash	$ 90,500	$ 64,700
Marketable securities	75,000	60,000
Accounts receivable (net)	115,000	120,000
Total	$280,500	$244,700
Current liabilities	$210,000	$243,000
Acid-test ratio	1.3	1.0

Use: To indicate instant debt-paying ability.

Which is the better ratio; the current ratio or the acid-test ratio?

Notes:

Solvency Measures — The Short-Term Creditor

Accounts Receivable Turnover

	2000	1999
Net sales on account	$1,498,000	$1,200,000
Accounts receivable (net):		
Beginning of year	$ 120,000	$ 140,000
End of year	115,000	120,000
Total	$ 235,000	$ 260,000
Average	$ 117,500	$ 130,000
Accts. receivable turnover	12.7	9.2

Use: To assess the efficiency in collecting
receivables and in the management of credit.

Number of Days' Sales in Receivables

	2000	1999
Accounts receivable (net)		
end of year	$ 115,000	$ 120,000
Net sales on account	$1,498,000	$1,200,000
Average daily sales on		
account (sales ÷ 365)	$ 4,104	$ 3,288
Number of days' sales in		
receivables	28	36.5

What could account
for the significant
improvement in the
collection days?

Use: To assess the efficiency in collecting
receivables and in the management of credit.

Notes:

Solvency Measures — The Short-Term Creditor

Inventory Turnover

	2000	1999
Cost of goods sold	$1,043,000	$ 820,000
Inventories:		
Beginning of year	$ 283,000	$ 311,000
End of year	264,000	283,000
Total	$ 547,000	$ 594,000
Average	$ 273,500	$ 297,000
Inventory turnover	**3.8**	**2.8**

Use: To assess the efficiency in the management of inventory.

Number of Days' Sales in Inventory

	2000	1999
Inventories, end of year	$ 264,000	$283,000
Cost of goods sold	$1,043,000	$820,000
Average daily cost of goods sold (COGS ÷ 365)	$ 2,858	$ 2,247
Number of days' sales in inventory	**92.4**	**125.9**

What could account for the significant improvement in the selling period?

Use: To assess the efficiency in the management of inventory.

Notes:

Solvency Measures — The Long-Term Creditor

Ratio of Fixed Assets to Long-Term Liabilities

	2000	1999
Fixed assets (net)	$444,500	$470,000
Long-term liabilities	$100,000	$200,000
Ratio of fixed assets to long-term liabilities	4.4	2.4

Does this really matter to the long-term creditor?

Use: To indicate the margin of safety to long-term creditors.

Ratio of Liabilities to Stockholders' Equity

	2000	1999
Total liabilities	$310,000	$443,000
Total stockholders' equity	$829,500	$787,500
Ratio of liabilities to stockholders' equity	0.37	0.56

Use: To indicate the margin of safety to creditors.

Number of Times Interest Charges Earned

	2000	1999
Income before income tax	$ 900,000	$ 800,000
Add interest expense	300,000	250,000
Amount available for interest	$1,200,000	$1,050,000
Number of times earned	4.0	4.2

Use: To assess the risk to debtholders in terms of number of times interest charges were earned.

Profitability Analysis

Profitability is the ability of an entity to earn profits.

This ability to earn profits depends on the effectiveness and efficiency of operations as well as resources available.

Profitability analysis focuses primarily on the relationship between operating results reported in the income statement and resources reported in the balance sheet.

Profitability Measures — The Common Stockholder

Ratio of Net Sales to Assets

	2000	1999
Net sales	$1,498,000	$1,200,000
Total assets:		
Beginning of year	$1,053,000	$1,010,000
End of year	1,044,500	1,053,000
Total	$2,097,500	$2,063,000
Average	$1,048,750	$1,031,500
Ratio of net sales to assets	1.4	1.2

Is this ratio also called asset turnover?

Use: To assess the effectiveness of the use of assets.

Notes:

Profitability Measures — The Common Stockholder

Rate Earned on Total Assets

	2000	1999
Net income	$ 91,000	$ 76,500
Plus interest expense	6,000	12,000
Total	$ 97,000	$ 88,500
Total assets:		
Beginning of year	$1,230,500	$1,187,500
End of year	1,139,500	1,230,500
Total	$2,370,000	$2,418,000
Average	$1,185,000	$1,209,000
Rate earned on total assets	8.2%	7.3%

Use: To assess the profitability of the assets.

Rate Earned on Stockholders' Equity

	2000	1999
Net income	$ 91,000	$ 76,500
Stockholders' equity:		
Beginning of year	$ 787,500	$ 750,000
End of year	829,500	787,500
Total	$1,617,000	$1,537,500
Average	$ 808,500	$ 768,750
Rate earned on equity	11.3%	10.0%

Use: To assess the profitability of the investment by stockholders.

Notes:

Profitability Measures — The Common Stockholder

Rate Earned on Common Stockholders' Equity

	2000	1999
Net income	$ 91,000	$ 76,500
Less preferred dividends	9,000	9,000
Remainder—common stock	$ 82,000	$ 67,500
Common stockholders' equity:		
Beginning of year	$ 637,500	$ 600,000
End of year	679,500	637,500
Total	$1,317,000	$1,237,500
Average	$ 658,500	$ 618,750
Rate earned on common equity	12.5%	10.9%

Use: To assess the profitability of the investment by common stockholders.

Earnings Per Share on Common Stock

	2000	1999
Net income	$ 91,000	$ 76,500
Less preferred dividends	9,000	9,000
Remainder—common stock	$ 82,000	$ 67,500
Shares of common stock	50,000	50,000
Earnings per share on common	$1.64	$1.35

Use: To assess the profitability of the investment by common stockholders.

Notes:

Profitability Measures — The Common Stockholder

Price-Earnings Ratio

	2000	19969
Market price per share of common	$20.50	$13.50
Earnings per share on common	$ 1.64	$ 1.35
Price-earnings ratio on common	12.5	10.0

Use: To indicate future earnings prospects, based on the relationship between market value of common stock and earnings.

Dividend Yield

	2000	1999
Dividends per share of common	$ 0.80	$ 0.60
Market price per share of common	$20.50	$13.50
Dividend yield on common stock	3.9%	4.4%

Use: To indicate the rate of return to common stockholders in terms of dividends.

Corporate Annual Reports

In addition to financial statements the annual report includes:

1. Financial Highlights
2. President's Letter to the Stockholders
3. Management Report
4. Independent Auditors' Report
5. Historical Summary

True / False Questions

True   False

_____ _____   1. The percentage analysis of increases and decreases in corresponding items in comparative financial statements is referred to as horizontal analysis.

_____ _____   2. Statements in which all items are expressed as percentages are called common-size statements.

_____ _____   3. Factors which reflect the ability of a business to pay its debts and earn a reasonable amount of income are referred to as equity and leverage.

_____ _____   4. The excess of current assets over current liabilities is referred to as working capital.

_____ _____   5. The ratio of current assets to current liabilities is referred to as the acid-test ratio.

_____ _____   6. If a firm has a current ratio of 2, the subsequent receipt of a 60-day note receivable on account will cause the ratio to decrease.

_____ _____   7. The number of days' sales in receivables is one means of expressing the relationship between credit sales and accounts receivable.

_____ _____   8. The number of days' sales in inventory is one means of expressing the relationship between the cost of goods sold and inventory.

_____ _____   9. An increase in the ratio of stockholders' equity to liabilities indicates an improvement in the margin of safety for creditors.

_____ _____   10. The rate earned on total common stockholders' equity for most thriving businesses will be higher than the rate earned on total assets.

_____ _____   11. The rate earned on current assets is one of the measures of solvency.

_____ _____   12. Ratios and various other analytical measures are not a substitute for sound judgment, nor do they provide definitive guides for action.

_____ _____   13. The effects of differences in accounting methods are of little importance when analyzing comparable data from competing businesses.

Instructions:

Place a check mark in the appropriate column.

Multiple Choice Questions

_____ 1. The percentage of change in long-term liabilities between two balance sheet dates is an example of:
   a. vertical analysis   b. solvency analysis
   c. profitability analysis   d. horizontal analysis

_____ 2. The ability of a business to pay its debts as they come due and to earn a reasonable amount of income is referred to as:
   a. solvency and leverage   b. solvency and profitability
   c. solvency and liquidity   d. solvency and equity

_____ 3. Which of the following is not an analysis used in assessing solvency?
   a. Inventory analysis   b. Number of times interest charges are earned
   c. Asset turnover   d. Accounts receivable analysis

_____ 4. A company with working capital of $400,000 and a current ratio of 2.5 pays a $50,000 short-term liability. The amount of working capital immediately after payment is:
   a. $250,000   b. $350,000   c. $400,000   d. $50,000

_____ 5. The tendency of the rate earned on stockholders' equity to vary disproportionately from the rate earned on total assets is sometimes referred to as:
   a. leverage   b. solvency   c. yield   d. quick assets

_____ 6. For most profitable companies, the rate earned on stockholders' equity will be less than:
   a. the rate earned on total assets
   b. the rate earned on total liabilities and stockholders' equity
   c. the rate earned on sales
   d. the rate earned on common stockholders' equity

_____ 7. Corporate annual reports typically do not contain which of the following:
   a. Financial highlights   b. SEC statement expressing an opinion
   c. Management report   d. Historical summary

Instructions:
Enter the letter of the best answer in the space provided.